TV and Film Toys and Ephemera

CROWOOD COLLECTORS' SERIES

TV and Film Toys and Ephemera

ARTHUR WARD

THE CROWOOD PRESS

First published in 2007 by
The Crowood Press Ltd
Ramsbury, Marlborough
Wiltshire SN8 2HR

www.crowood.com

British Library Cataloguing-in-Publication Data
A catalogue record for this book is available from the British Library.

ISBN 978 1 86126 926 3

All photography by Arthur Ward.

Acknowledgements
I would like to thank the following people for allowing me to borrow items so that I could photograph them and put them in this book: Martel Mitchell for the loan of World Cup Willie and Orinoco Womble. Nigel Gray for the loan of his Fireball XL5 cards. Simon Armstrong for the loan of the *Dad's Army* annual.

Typeset and designed by
D & N Publishing
Lambourn Woodlands, Hungerford, Berkshire.

Printed and bound in India by Replika Press.

DEDICATION

To my daughters, Eleanor and Alice. This book shows you why I bought all those old toys and what I did with them. Perhaps you will understand why I didn't let you play with them, girls. Read the book carefully, because one day they will all be yours!

Also to Tamara, with love. Thanks for all your patience and encouragement; it kept me going!

Last but by no means least to Bronte, who must have wondered what on earth was going on as, night after night, electronic flashlight lit up the garden outside the kitchen window!

Well, girls, I hope you like the results.

Alice

Eleanor

Bronte

PREFACE

This book is principally aimed at collectors of film- and television-inspired toys. It is my humble intention either simply to remind you of the things you enjoyed before adult pressures took hold, or, if you're a collector like me, show you what's worth collecting and tell you how to go about it.

Collecting anything is hard work. It eats up cash that could be used for more pressing matters. It consumes free time. It engenders obsessive behaviour and encourages friends to question one's hold on reality. And ultimately it can be unfulfilling as few collectors have *everything* they 'need' and anyway the never-ending quest for sought-after objects often becomes an end in itself.

However, any collection that provides pleasure and profit can't be all bad, can it? The pursuit of fine paintings and fifteenth-century Chinese porcelain, for example, has long delivered prizes to enthusiasts. But they have to be rich ones.

This book is aimed at ordinary, everyday collectors who have to juggle the finances to satisfy their harmless indulgence – specifically, as collectors of post-war toys.

Fortunately, old toys have significantly appreciated in value during the past couple of decades and although toy collectables aren't in the same league as Grand Masters, the values attributed by dealers to old Dinky Toys, Action Men, early 007 toys and first-generation *Star Wars* figures bears little relation to their original cost (encouraging that oft-heard phrase muttered through gritted teeth, 'I had one of those!'). And how much fun can you really have with a Canaletto compared to an Imperial Storm Trooper mounted on a miniature Speeder Bike?

Enjoy…

**ARTHUR WARD,
Houghton, West Sussex,
September 2006**

1945: PEACE AND THE POST-WAR BABY BOOM

I suppose every generation thinks it's got it made. Despite the fact that those of us born between 1946 and 1964, defined as 'baby boomers' by sociologists, aren't whizzing around on the personal hovercrafts promised by the magazines of our youth, we're still having it pretty good.

Those of us born since the end of World War Two have experienced some of the most seismic changes in modern history. Weaned on early television and growing up beneath the over-arching threat of nuclear Armageddon, we developed in parallel with the nascent space industry and its promise of exciting new horizons. In Vietnam, we saw the first war that television reported and, arguably, stopped.

However, whether we actually 'matured' during this period of enormous change is debatable. Readers of this book are either interested in, or collect, old toys. This desire to reach for the security blanket of our childhood is curious, to say the least. But I don't care. *Mea culpa* – I love old toys. I relish the past and happily wallow in my private nostalgia. Why not? Life's too short. There's plenty of time to worry about mundane stuff like jobs, paying the bills and familial responsibility.

So instead of maturing, perhaps we simply 'seasoned'. Thankfully, however, we never forgot the excitement of the toys, plastic kits and board games we played with as youngsters.

There's one main problem with the modern collectors' lot, however. Today, many years after we quite naturally threw away our Action Men, Dinkys and Meccano sets, we want them back. Amazingly, although many of them can still be found, they cost an awful lot more than they did when first available.

Of course, one of the things that has transformed the lot of those of us who collect things is the World Wide Web. I don't remember any of the wise sages of yesteryear predicting this. It seems to have crept under the wire whilst we 'boomers' were transfixed by images of Apollo missions and satisfied by the technological transition from vinyl to compact disc.

Although many of today's most collectable toys have been inspired by the prevailing film and TV culture, it would be wrong to assume that spin-off toy merchandise is purely a product of the so-called TV generations. Well before the advent of the cathode-ray tube, existing media encouraged childhood games of war, cowboys and Indians, or space travel. Prior to the contemporary 'tie-in' phenomenon, characterized by the licensed arrangements associated with the 007 or *Thunderbirds* franchises in the 1960s and perfected by George Lucas's groundbreaking *Star Wars* merchandise deals, entertainment vehicles like 'the pictures' (cinema), 'the wireless' (radio) and comics influenced fertile minds.

The Wireless Leads the Way

As with most things, the revolution in the marketing of toys via cinema and radio began in the United States. There, the first really successful children's premiums were inspired by popular radio shows. On 7 November 1932, three years after it was first printed in comic format, one of the most popular serials, *Buck Rogers in the 25th Century*, could be heard for the first time on radio. Every day, Buck and his liberated co-pilot Wilma Deering, together with the brilliant Dr Huer, kept the world safe.

Evidence of the programme's phenomenal success was the incredible response to mail-order gifts that were

offered to listeners. For example, an initial offering of a map of the planets brought 125,000 requests. Because of this massive response, a subsequent offering of a cardboard space helmet was made more difficult to obtain. It required listeners to mail a metal seal from a can of Cocomalt, which took over from Kellogg's as the show's sponsor in 1935. Nevertheless, despite being in the midst of the Great Depression, children still managed to

LEFT: *Film Fun The "Kinema Comic"*, 15 May 1920. This weekly comic, the forerunner of the better-known *TV Comic*, was first published in 1920 (a very early edition is shown). The featured cover story concerns Ben Turpin and Charlie Lynn, two comics from the Mack Sennett stable. *Film Fun* survived until 1962.

BELOW: Double-page spread from the 15 May 1920 edition of *Film Fun*.

send in more than 140,000 strips of tin – so desirable was the premium. This has since become an extremely rare and valuable collectors' item. Some of the other popular items from the series' lifetime were rings, including three especially collectable ones: the Dragon's Eye, Blue Coal and Saturn rings.

From 1936, other sponsors, such as Cream of Wheat and Popsicle, took up the mantle. The *Buck Rogers* radio show was sponsored until it came to an end in 1947.

In Britain, the Ovaltineys championed a popular malt bedtime drink that first arrived in Britain from Switzerland in 1913 but reached the height of its popularity in the 1930s. The Ovaltineys became so popular that, beginning in 1935, they had their own Radio Luxembourg show on Sunday evenings. The Ovaltineys even had their own insert in the popular children's comic, *Rocket*.

Millions of children joined the League of Ovaltineys and were issued with cards, badges and secret codes. Youngsters proudly wore their Ovaltineys badges to school – considering them of a higher status than those saying 'Prefect'.

Traditionally, some of the most popular radio premiums featured 'decoding' mechanisms, which children needed to send off for so that they could work out 'secret' messages. Ovaltine is enormously popular in the United States, and as recently as 2000, in return for two proof-of-purchases and $2.50, consumers of the brand could send away for a decoder that could be worn as a ring. It should be noted that in the USA, decoder pins and badges especially have long been popular. Collectors especially value those associated with the *Little Orphan Annie* radio show, which used to feature an Ovaltine commercial before the start of every programme and another one at the end.

The other hugely successful children's show of the 1930s and 40s, on both sides of the Atlantic, was *The Lone Ranger*. It first appeared on US station WXYZ in Detroit in January 1933. Merchandising for the show began in earnest in 1938 but really took off after 1941 when General Mills became the sponsor. Incidentally, keen readers will recognize the name of this massive US conglomerate. It rescued Airfix from receivership in

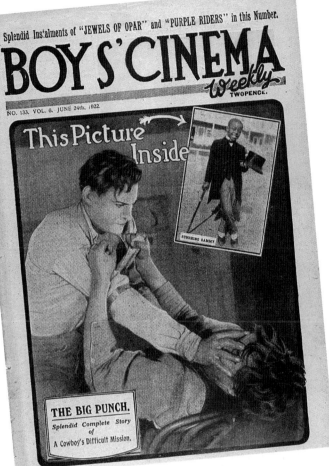

Boys' Cinema Weekly from June 1922. A free picture of 'Sunshine Sammy Morrison', one of the earliest 'Our Gang' members, could be found inside.

1981, installing the British kit company within its British subsidiary, Palitoy. In the 1940s and 1950s General Mills' brands, such as Kix, Cheerios and Wheaties, sponsored *The Lone Ranger*, distributing various premiums, one of the most collectable of which was 'The Lone Ranger Frontier Town'. This exciting premium was huge, featuring a base layout that covered 15 square feet and could be completed by the addition of a variety of buildings that could be sent for in return for a box lid and a 'dime'. As the radio show featured stories centred on Frontier Town, listeners could play along with their own replicas of the settlement featured on the radio.

Dick Tracy was another classic radio series, which originated in America but soon developed a loyal fan base in Britain. It began in 1935 on the Mutual Broadcasting System, a cooperative venture formed by existing stations from New York, Chicago, Cincinnati and Detroit as an alternative to NBC and CBS, the existing national networks. However, it soon transferred to NBC, going nationwide and crossing the Atlantic at the same time.

The most coveted premium given away with breakfast cereal required real brand loyalty. Kids had to munch their way through thirty-nine boxes of Quaker Puffed Wheat before they were awarded the prized Dick Tracy Inspector General badge.

Britain's home-grown answer to *Dick Tracy* was another Dick: *Dick Barton – Special Agent*. This private investigator and sometime special agent was the star of the BBC's first daily radio serial, appearing in 711 episodes between 1946 and 1951. At its peak, over 15 million listeners tuned in to hear Barton's adventures, broadcast in the early evening, right after the news. Not surprisingly, comics, commercial sponsors and toy companies jumped at the chance to ally themselves with a name attracting so much interest from young people. Toys and premiums abounded.

In Britain, *Dick Barton* and other popular shows such as *Jennings at School* and *Norman and Henry Bones* were heard on *Children's Hour*, the BBC's popular radio show that ran from 1924 to 1964. The programme had been a solace to parents and children during the dark days of the war years, but it reached its zenith when presented by 'Uncle Mac' Derek McCulloch, in the early 1950s.

Not surprisingly, the return of the BBC Television Service in 1946 (it had been turned off during the war years) enabled children to see and want to copy favourite characters exactly. The increasing audiences gave a huge boost to replica toys and games based on TV heroes. Commercial television, with the added fillip of advertisements for products related to the characters, provided another massive boost when it arrived in 1955, nineteen years after the BBC's regular schedule of programmes had begun.

An early character was *Mr Pastry*, who first appeared on British television in 1946 and had his own series into the early 1960s, played by the moustachioed actor

OPPOSITE PAGE:

TOP: 'Muffin the Mule' – arguably British TV's first children's superstar.

BOTTOM: Back pages of Britain's *T.V. Fun* from the 1950s. 007 fans will notice a feature about Shirley Eaton. She was already a celebrity in the 1950s, but achieved international fame when she was painted gold in the Sean Connery 007 feature *Goldfinger* in 1964.

Richard Hearne (who incidentally was at one time considered as the replacement for the *Doctor Who* actor William Hartnell). In the mid 1950s, British company Mettoy produced a now very collectable 'Mr. Pastry Pop Apart Target Game'.

In the next chapter, we will look at the development of children's television of the 1950s and its influence on toy manufacturers to produce items based on TV characters.

It was fortunate that a new medium, plastic, arrived to enable toy manufacturers to create cheap, bright playthings quickly enough to distribute them in time to capitalize on the popularity of successful children's radio. Demand also increased towards the end of the 1940s due to the expanding audience of BBC television's *Watch With Mother*.

The Advent of Plastic

Just as the post-war baby boom was a result of so many fit young men returning to their wives and girlfriends from overseas service in World War Two, so the mass-production techniques, which heralded the age of plastic and enabled the cheap and efficient production of toys, were also a direct result of that conflict.

The years 1939–45 saw unprecedented technological developments. For example, when the Nazis invaded Poland in 1939, the RAF's front-line strength included biplanes; when the war ended, Fighter Command had jet-engined fighter-bombers in its squadrons. At the beginning of the war, anti-aircraft shells were fused to detonate at a predetermined height and the guns were laid by eye aided by complex mechanical

calculators. By the war's end, rapid-firing AA guns hit their targets with the aid of radar and proximity fuses in each shell. The myriad new weapons components in use, especially those used in avionics equipment, necessitated new production techniques so that dials, switches, junction boxes, fascias, microphones and headsets could be mass-produced and moulded in synthetic materials such as plastics.

Combined, the developments in miniaturization, electronics, synthetics, die-cutting and pattern-making required to support the war efforts of all the warring nations meant that the peace dividend brought massive commercial opportunities for commercial manufacturers of all kinds. Not least toy makers.

However, before the toy industry settled on the ubiquitous polystyrene-based plastics that all children take for granted today, manufacturers had pioneered countless alternative polymers. For example, Edwardian toy manufacturers experimented with a range of materials based on nitrocellulose compounds. In 1870 in the United States, the Hyatt brothers invented Celluloid as a suitable material for billiard balls. Shortly afterwards, in 1872, the Smith & Lock company patented the first injection-moulding machine in an attempt to hasten the manufacture of mass-moulded items. Unfortunately, the then available plastic proved unsuitable for the new process and Smith & Lock's revolutionary machine would have to wait until a different raw material was synthesized.

Germany, rapidly becoming a major player in the chemical and dyestuffs arena, also had a fledgling toy industry and was particularly advanced in the production of tin-plate items. German toy makers also turned to new methods in synthetic and composite production that were a by-product of their chemical industry. In 1919, Germany at last produced a thermally stable cellulose plastic – cellulose acetate.

A revised injection-moulding process was invented, the most famous system being that patented by the American Leo Baekeland, inventor of the famous phenol-formaldehyde resin/plastic, Bakelite. Readers might be interested to learn that Bayko, an enormously popular construction toy in Britain during the 1930s, was made from a derivative of that wonder Art Deco plastic. It is worth noting that although today's

polystyrene injection-moulding machines are far more sophisticated, their principal mechanisms would not be unfamiliar to the early American and German pioneers of such technology.

By the 1940s, the developments in plastics that had taken place pre-war were given further impetus by Japan's speedy conquest of Anglo-Dutch possessions in the Far East. These brought a halt to Britain and America's ready supply of latex. The result was a range of truly synthetic products, many of which were based on acetates, that predated the advent of polystyrene.

Since the war, most people have associated plastic with scale-model construction kits and it's true their development has helped to encourage perfections in the injection moulding of toys, which has been essential to the modern industry. But while most people in the UK tend to think of Airfix as being the oldest home-grown plastic kit manufacturer, in fact that honour goes to another British manufacturer – FROG.

FROG 'Penguins' were manufactured exclusively from the earliest synthetic plastic material then commercially available. The name FROG was already well established by the mid 1930s. In fact, the 'Flies Right Off the Ground' brand dates back to 1932.

Penguins, however, were the first 'proper' plastic construction kits and they also came from IMA, the owners of FROG. Penguins were true scale replicas and were intended to be painstakingly assembled and painted, then displayed on shelves or in glass cabinets indoors. Unlike previous FROG aircraft, however, these birds couldn't fly. Consequently, Penguin was considered the ideal brand name!

FROG Penguins first appeared in the shops during Christmas 1936. They were manufactured from cellulose acetate butyrate, one of the new thermoplastics that were beginning to emerge from laboratories in the 1930s. Cellulose acetate material possessed excellent moulding qualities and was far more stable than its sister material – the highly inflammable staple of the early film industry, cellulose nitrate, the plastic that encouraged the urgent development of 'safety film'.

Modern kits are manufactured from injection-moulded polystyrene. This thermoplastic was developed alongside the acetate family in the 1930s, but although the first plastic injection-moulding machine had been patented in Germany in 1926, it wasn't until immediately after World War Two that polystyrene injection-moulding technology became widely available.

Throughout the war years, plastics were generally only used by the armed forces of the belligerents, mainly by the British and Germans for military communications in headsets and microphones. Real, rather than model, aircraft consumed a great deal of plastic material. A plethora of switches, knobs and dials festooned the cockpits and radio positions of fighters and bombers and most of these devices were made from synthetics. The fascias of the new cathode ray (radar) instruments, which had recently been adopted by rival air forces, were also predominantly assembled from plastic mouldings. Wartime development, combined with the loss of the raw materials for rubber production to advancing Japanese armies as they overran Allied rubber plantations, further encouraged the rapid transition from vulcanized natural materials to true synthetics. The plastic age as we know it really started with the coming of peace in 1945.

Ironically, the discovery and capture of German manufacturing plant at the war's end was a further encouragement. Even more starved of raw materials than Britain, Nazi Germany had been forced to accelerate the development of plastics manufacture. With a tradition of inventiveness and having perfected some leading-edge production processes, the Third Reich was also in the van of injection moulding.

As the conscripted Allied armies advanced on the shattered country, many over-curious former engineers took advantage of the opportunities presented by so much abandoned plant. Rather unscrupulously perhaps, details of German innovation and, allegedly, complete injection-moulding machines found their way back to Britain and America, forming the basis of both nations' post-war plastics industry.

Apart from providing the impetus for new and more efficient production techniques, World War II was a catalyst for the emerging post-war toy industry in other ways.

The rapid developments in military technology, especially in aviation – the modern jet engine came of age during the 1939–45 conflict – provided a huge range of new subjects for toy manufacturers. This was

especially true for manufacturers of die-cast vehicles like Dinky, which, although its range had contained a variety of aircraft since its inception in 1933, realized the potential of adding replicas of war planes and the new civil airliners to catalogues full of racing and saloon cars and chunky commercial vehicles.

Dozens of blockbuster war films, books and magazines provided all the raw material required to stimulate fertile young imaginations. The stories of real life-heroes like Audie Murphy, Douglas Bader and Captain Walker RN encouraged a demand for a whole range of playthings centred on military vehicles, such as ships and fighter planes. The furious pace for toys based on the latest machine inventions was later exacerbated by the Cold War and the space race. *Sputnik* and the pioneering American rocket-propelled X-Planes spawned dozens of tin and plastic toys and scores of different model kits and board games.

Post-war, increasing demand for toys, together with manufacturers' new-found facility for mass production in synthetics, led to a relocation of centres of production. This move was designed to take advantage of cheaper labour and far less rigorous employment laws. Consequently, manufacturing bases were established most notably in Hong Kong, followed by Taiwan and Korea.

Today, many of the cheap plastic toys and novelties from Hong Kong, often derided by domestic consumers weaned on the tough alloys of Meccano, Dinky and Britain's, are highly sought after. Post-war Japan had a thriving tin-plate toy industry, which had picked up the remnants of successful pre-war enterprises prior to the redevelopment and investment that spawned a burgeoning electronics sector, but Hong Kong was the plastics king. Where would brands like Marx, Timpo, Bachmann, Gilbert and Cherilea, for example, have been without a source of cheap production? Certainly, those children of the 1950s and 1960s, who shook the premiums from their breakfast cereal boxes, wouldn't have enjoyed such regular 'free' gifts with their cornflakes if the likes of Kellogg's and Nabisco had been unable to source such cheap premiums. Another reason to thank the much-derided Hong Kong plastics industry, and more or less where we came in!

In 1955 Peter Dimmock did the sports presenter job that Gary Lineker does today.

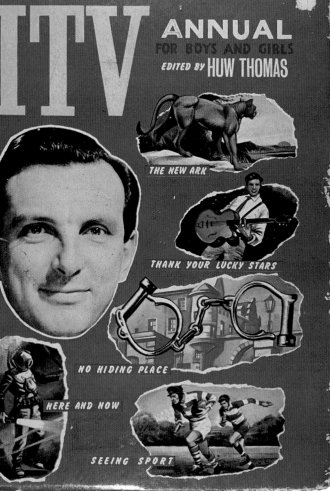

From 1955, this annual was edited by Huw Thomas, who was one of British Independent Television's (ITV) first newsreaders, along with Robin Day, Reginald Bosanquet and Ludovic Kennedy.

THE 1950s: TOP TV, THE BIG MOVIES, MEDIA EVENTS

The late, great comedian Barry Took once wrote,

> Television before 1955 had contained very little of note – at least that I can remember. It was still very much the 'little brother' of radio and was watched by only a tiny minority. What's more, at that time the TV day was very short: an hour of programmes in the afternoon aimed at women, children's television between 5.00 and 6.00pm and then close down until 7.30 when the service resumed with the news and weather. After an evening of plays, variety and talks, close down came at 10.30 with the news in 'sound only'.

Uncle Mac story books are now becoming increasingly rare and collectable.

In 1955 the BBC, which had enjoyed a monopoly since it became the world's first broadcaster of what was then high-definition television (over 200 lines) in 1936, pausing its services for security reasons during World War Two, faced, for the first time, competition: Independent Television (ITV) was born. The BBC was forced to up its game.

This new pressure to capture the largest share of the audience was particularly good news for children.

Derek McCulloch, 'Uncle Mac' of BBC radio fame, had been a childhood constant since the war years. Even with the advent of TV his privileged place in the nation's heart was assured.

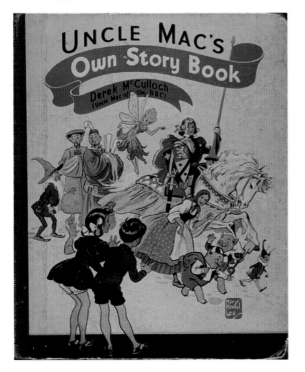

There's nothing like competition and market pressure to improve product quality. As Barry Took continued:

> Evening television was lost to me as I was working in the theatre, but I do remember children's television. Stamped on my mind is *All Your Own* with Huw Wheldon hectoring talented if nervous, child performers like a sergeant major with a row of new recruits. I also remember Humphry Lestocq with the bad-tempered puppet Mr. Turnip; Annette Mills with the well-behaved Muffin the Mule and his friends Peregrine the Penguin and Willy the Worm dancing around on her piano top…. All very safe and cosy.

It All Began with Puppets

Muffin the Mule was the first really famous British children's television character. His popularity further encouraged his immortalization in countless toys and books. Although Muffin is quite naturally associated with Annette Mills, who appeared with him on television as early as 1946, the equine superstar actually predated his association with the famous presenter.

In fact, Muffin first hit the boards as one of the Hogarth Puppets, the husband and wife partnership Anne Hogarth and Jan Bussell who toured Britain in the interwar years with a range of puppets featuring clowns and other characters displaying a variety of stage antics. Muffin was conceived in 1933 when Jan Bussell scribbled the outline of a mule, literally on the back of an envelope, and asked a traditional Punch & Judy puppet maker (Fred Tickner) to manufacture an articulated version to pep up their show.

Annette Mills, sister of screen actor John, was already establishing a career as a performer on *Children's Hour* when, early in 1946, she visited Anne Hogarth's home, asking her if she had any puppets suitable for her show. She immediately chose the as yet unnamed mule puppet and promptly named him 'Muffin', quickly penning the classic verse 'We want Muffin, Muffin the Mule…'. He first appeared with Annette in an episode of *For the Children*. The rest is history.

As far as Muffin toys are concerned, probably the most well known are the countless puppet and marionette replicas of the star himself. However, such was the merchandising industry surrounding him that a variety of games, including superb card games dating to the late 1940s – all copyright 'The Muffin Syndicate' – regularly turn up at toy auctions today commanding

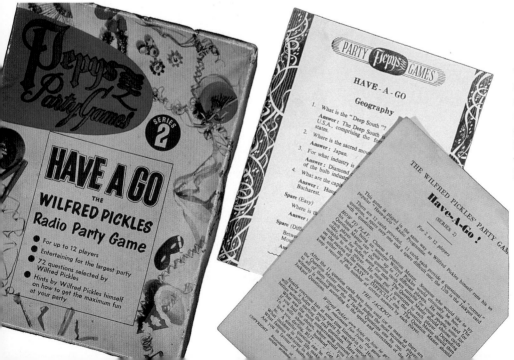

Wilfred Pickles' radio show *Have a Go* was on air between 1946 until 1967. This party game version of the hit show enabled fans to play at their leisure.

1950s Muffin the Mule Junior finger puppet manufactured by Britain's 'MOKO'. Keen enthusiasts will know that early Matchbox toys were often classified 'A MOKO Lesney', MOKO standing for one of the firm's earliest distributor/partners, Moses Kohnstam. His grandson, Richard, is well known amongst modellers as the original distributor of Japanese Tamiya construction kits in Britain.

premium prices. The *My Annette Mills Gift Book*, published in 1953 and featuring Muffin the Mule, Prudence Kitten, Charlie Parking and Colonel Crock, proved enormously popular and was a bestseller. In 1948, British manufacturer EVB Plastics produced a personal favourite of mine: the Beeju Muffin the Mule Toy TV Set.

In concert with Muffin the Mule, the other big star of children's television in the medium's earliest days was Mr. Turnip, star of BBC television's Saturday afternoon children's show *Whirligig*, first broadcast in November 1950. Alongside puppets Hank the Cowboy and his goofy horse Old Timer (surely the models for Pixar's Woody and Bullseye from *Toy Story*?), the unpleasant Mr. Turnip and his stooge Humphrey Lestocq ('HL' to devotees of the show) more than satisfied children of the pre Gerry Anderson generation.

As with Muffin the Mule, a variety of manufacturers naturally produced replica puppets, enabling children to present their own performances complete with myriad individual pronunciations of Mr. Turnip's catchphrase, 'Lawky, Lawky, Lum'. A variety of *Mr. Turnip* and *Whirligig* annuals added to the available children's merchandise. However, some of the rarest surviving toys are those featuring pieces that could be most easily lost like Mr. Turnip's Aerial Ring Game, which required players to score points by hooking plastic rings on numbered protuberances sticking out of Mr. Turnip's body.

Mr. Turnip vied with Muffin the Mule for top spot in the hearts of children in 1950s Britain. Most youngsters preferred the benign mule to the grumpy vegetable.

OPPOSITE ABOVE: Readers could follow the hilarious adventures of 1950s TV celebrities such as Arthur Askey in the 1950s weekly, *T.V. Fun*.

OPPOSITE BELOW LEFT: *T.V. Fun Annual* from 1957 with young stars Shirley Eaton (of the James Bond film *Goldfinger* fame), Terry Scott and Bill Maynard on the cover.

OPPOSITE BELOW RIGHT: This *TV Fun Annual* from 1958 features cover star of the weekly comic, Arthur Askey, in pride of place.

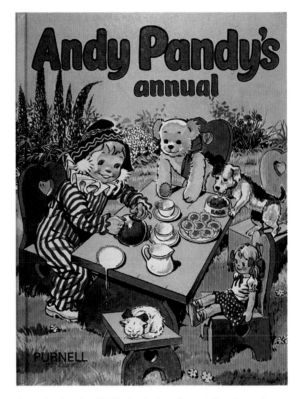

Amazingly, the BBC's *Andy Pandy* was first broadcast in 1950. This annual is from the early 1960s.

On 21 May 1950 the BBC's famous Lime Grove TV studios opened. These studios, originally occupied by Gaumont, Gainsborough and Rank Films, dated to 1915. They were home to lots of children's TV programmes including *Doctor Who* and *Blue Peter*. The first BBC children's newsreel was also broadcast in 1950. Sadly, Lime Grove Studios were closed in 1992 and later demolished to make way for residential housing. Many of the programmes were subsequently transferred to the BBC's Television Centre that had opened in White City in 1960.

Another staple of the earliest children's television was *Andy Pandy*, first televised on 11 July 1950 and repeated so often during the following fifty years that most people assume it dates from the 1960s at the earliest. Andy was accompanied by his friends Teddy and Looby Loo (who in those very non-PC days used to sweep the dust from Andy's house, when she wasn't singing her catchphrase, 'Here We Go Looby Loo', or consigned to return to her basket).

Most of those involved in early BBC television had naturally gained their spurs in radio, up to then the biggest and most powerful broadcast medium in the world. In fact, Freda Lingstrom, the originator of *Andy Pandy*, had previously worked on radio's *Listen With Mother*. *Andy Pandy* was her response to a brief from BBC television executives to devise 'a television equivalent on music and movement lines' to the sort of material she had produced for radio. Turning to her long-time friend Maria Bird, the pair devised the 'three-year-old' string puppet Andy, designed to talk and act rather like the show's toddler viewers; a kind of 1950s precursor to the *Teletubbies* a generation later.

Andy Pandy's popularity with young viewers encouraged toy manufacturers and publishers to grab every available licensing opportunity. Andy Pandy toys appeared in similar numbers to those produced of Mr. Turnip and Muffin. However, Andy Pandy was also the cover 'star' of *Robin*, the popular children's comic. Such was his acclaim that from his first appearance on the cover of *Robin* on 28 March 1953, the blue and white striped celebrity remained a fixture on a further 836 covers! Andy Pandy was also immortalized in glove puppet form. British toy manufacturer Chad Valley (*see below*) made at least two versions that I know of. One featured a moulded vinyl head and hands, while the other had fabric hands and a vinyl head. Both were dressed in Andy's familiar blue and white striped romper suit.

The Flowerpot Men, like *Andy Pandy*, was also created by Westerham Arts Films, Lingstrom and Bird's production company named after the Kent village in which it was based. In fact, Freda Lingstrom was also

Head of Children's Programmes for the BBC and in an enviable position to understand what young viewers wanted to watch … and to produce it for them.

Bill and Ben, the Flowerpot Men, were identical characters made entirely from flowerpots. They lived 'secretly' at the bottom of a farmer's garden (but had their names painted on their backs!). Though almost identical, they each had distinctly different voices. Should the farmer be approaching, a warning from their friend, Little Weed, would cause them to disappear quickly back into the safety of their terracotta pots.

At the time, a very popular piece of Flowerpot Men merchandise was British manufacturer Chad Valley's glove puppets of the duo. These toys featured velvet fabric plant pots kept rigid by the inclusion of a stout wire rim, the puppet being attached to the pot and operated via a hole in the pot base.

Shortly after *The Flowerpot Men* was first broadcast, it and stablemates *Andy Pandy* and *The Woodentops* were grouped together under the collective name, *Watch With Mother*.

In the days long before video recorders, 1950s children of pre-school age and much older could enjoy highlights of *Watch With Mother* programmes at leisure on their own piece of audio-visual equipment – a Chad Valley Give A Show projector which featured 112 slides of their heroes. The screen? The inside of the box lid, of course.

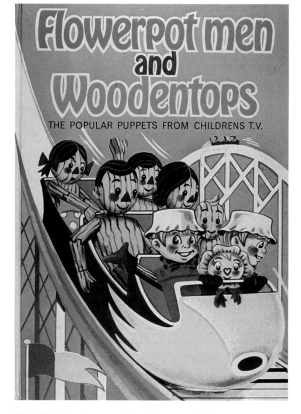

The Woodentops and **The Flowerpot Men** were brought to the screen by the same prodigious team that created **Muffin the Mule**. Together, they first appeared on Friday afternoon's **Watch With Mother** in 1955.

A BRIEF HISTORY OF CHAD VALLEY

The brand name 'Chad Valley' crops up time and again when discussing British 'TV Generation' toys and games. It was named after the stream flowing through the West Midlands village of Harborne, which was the location for founders Joseph and Alfred Johnson's stationery company that was incorporated in 1860, although the trademark 'Chad Valley' wasn't adopted until 1897. After patenting a stuffing machine for soft toys in 1916, the company became a real force in the manufacture of 'plush' toys in Britain. In 1938 Chad Valley received a British Royal Warrant, which read 'Toymakers to Her Majesty the Queen' until 1953 (the coronation of Queen Elizabeth II), when the wording was changed to 'Queen Mother'. In 1978 Chad Valley was taken over by Palitoy, the British company that later became part of the US giant Kenner Parker. The Chad Valley name lives on, however, albeit in Asia, following Woolworth's purchase of the name and manufacture of toys in that burgeoning economic region.

The aforementioned *Woodentops* was brought to the screen by the same prodigious team that created Muffin and the Flowerpot Men, and first appeared on Friday afternoon's *Watch With Mother* in 1955. Consisting of Daddy, Mummy, twins Jenny and Willy and Baby Woodentop, the family was supplemented by home-help Mrs Scrubbitt and Sam, who helped Daddy Woodentop in the garden. There was also Buttercup the cow and, of course, the real 'talent' of the line-up, the unforgettable Spotty Dog, always introduced as 'the biggest spotty dog you ever did see'.

Interestingly, in an online poll conducted by The Entertainer toy shop as recently as 2003, encouraging subscribers to vote for the return of vintage toys from their childhood, of the amazing 20,000 responses, Woodentops toys came in fifth place. Ironically, despite its success, *The Woodentops* never attracted any merchandise spin-offs. This just goes to show, as

one newspaper report recorded, that 'the fact that people wanted to buy reissues of toys that never existed in the first place perhaps tells us all we need to know about the power of nostalgia'.

Archie Andrews was another personality that effortlessly made the jump from radio to TV. Archie was the 'dummy' sidekick of ventriloquist Peter Brough. At its peak, the radio show, *Educating Archie*, could count on an impressive 15 million regular viewers and a fan club of a quarter-of-a-million children. Bit parts on the radio show were played by an impressive line-up of characters on the brink of superstardom, including Tony Hancock, Max Bygraves, Benny Hill, Beryl Reid and a fourteen-year-old Julie Andrews.

In the 1950s, scripts for the Archie Andrews TV shows were written by such emerging luminaries as Marty Feldman and Ronald Chesney and the programme also featured Irene Handl and Dick Emery.

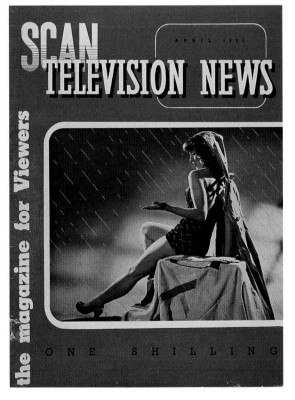

The cover of this early edition of *Scan Television News* features the kind of uninspiring composition early viewers were treated to.

The *Radio Fun Annuals* are now quite collectable. They were first produced in 1940, with the last appearing in 1960.

Although puppets were clearly all the rage amongst TV toys in the 1950s, puppets of Archie Andrews, himself a kind of puppet, were perhaps more appropriate. British manufacturer Palitoy was already a leading name in the production of toy dolls in the 1950s, so it was no surprise that the company obtained the licence to manufacture toy puppets of Archie, including a rather elaborate and now extremely rare (especially in its box) full body ventriloquist's doll, emblazoned with box art reading 'YOU Can Do It! and a smaller version of only Archie's head, the mouth of which could be snapped open and shut and the eyes made to roll by operating a lever beneath the toy's neck.

In 1948, having purchased a bear puppet on Blackpool Pier for 7s 6d to entertain his children, Harry Corbett will be forever associated with it. The puppet came to be known as Sooty. Sooty got his first break in 1952 as a regular feature on the BBC's children's TV programme, *Saturday Special*. His big break came in 1955 when the BBC first broadcast *The Sooty Show*. Almost immediately, there was a range of Sooty merchandise available, although his success really took off in the next decade when sex entered the bear's den with the addition of a girlfriend, Sue.

Cowboys and Indians

The adventures of a masked hero, the Lone Ranger, and Tonto, provided much of the film and TV entertainment for older children in the 1950s. In fact, the series kicked off in 1949 and between then and 1957 221 episodes of the exciting adventure serial were devoured as viewers followed the adventures of stars Clayton Moore and Jay Silverheels in stirring episodes with names such as 'The Legend of the Old Timers', 'The Lone Ranger Fights On' and 'Rifles and Renegades'.

Ventriloquist Terry Hall presented *The Lenny the Lion Show* between 1957 and 1960.

The Lone Ranger and Tonto were a big hit with children all over the world when the programme was broadcast between 1949 and 1957.

RIGHT: **William Lawrence Boyd – Hopalong Cassidy – and his horse Topper were the original post-war Wild West heroes.**

LEFT: **Born in 1911, the late Roy Rogers (he died in 1998) was known as 'King of the Cowboys' in the 1950s.**

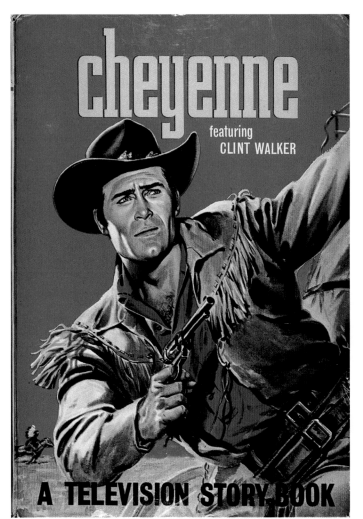

LEFT: *Cheyenne*, another of the almost ubiquitous Westerns on screen at the time, starred Clint Walker and was on air for a long time (1955–63).

RIGHT: Hollywood star Hugh O'Brian starred as Wyatt Earp on TV between 1955 and 1961. This British-made Bell Toys jigsaw puzzle has, remarkably, survived intact.

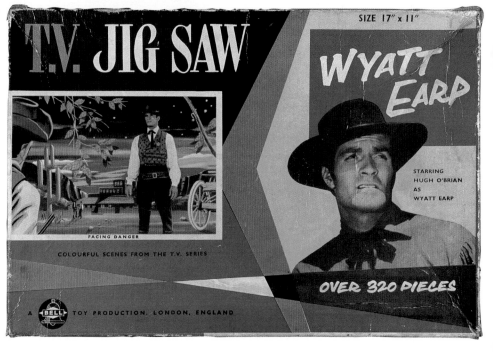

Royalty Reaches the Masses

Following the death of her father King George VI on 6 February 1952, the then Princess Elizabeth became the new heir to the British throne. The coronation of Her Majesty Queen Elizabeth II at Westminster Abbey on 2

June 1953 was not only one of the biggest media events of the decade, it was the single greatest stimulus to the increased adoption of television sets in Britain at the time. An estimated TV audience of more than 20 million viewers, almost double those who followed it on radio, watched the unfolding ceremony. For the first time in Britain, the viewers eclipsed listeners.

As a portent of the importance of the future baby boomers generation, 200 children at London's Great Ormond Street Hospital saw the coronation in colour, on a closed circuit linked to three state-of-the-art cameras overlooking Parliament Square.

Naturally, the market in patriotic souvenirs was enormous. That for toy representations of everything from Household Cavalrymen, Beefeaters and miniature crown jewels was equally significant. Perhaps one of the most popular toys then, and an enduring one with collectors today, was the gilded state coach manufactured by Lesney, the originators of the Matchbox range.

LEFT: *TV News* from 1953, coronation year. There wasn't much to watch, though, as the BBC enjoyed a monopoly in Britain until 1955.

BELOW: Queen Elizabeth's coronation was the first such event to be televised and it attracted an enormous audience. British kit manufacturer Paramount had a reputation for replicas of horse-drawn vehicles so it's little wonder that like so many other manufacturers they too produced a coronation souvenir.

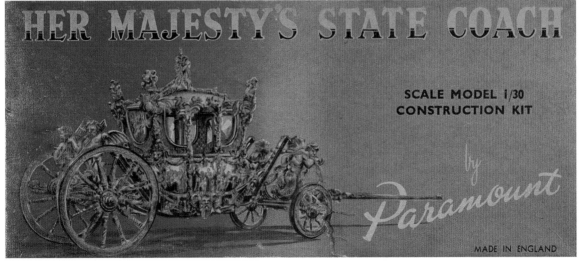

A BRIEF HISTORY OF MATCHBOX

The Matchbox brand originates from 1947 when two unrelated friends, Londoners Leslie and Rodney Smith, started the business they had long dreamt of. Their new company was called Lesney Products, a name that combined syllables from each of their forenames. Almost right from the start, the pair were joined by engineering designer John ('Jack') Odell, who quickly became Lesney's pattern and die-maker and was made a full partner in the new business.

Lesney is most famous for its Matchbox range of die-casts, the first of which, a large road-roller, was released in 1948. Made of 'mazac', a robust zinc alloy, Matchbox toys were virtually indestructible. However, it was the restrictions in the post-war rationing of zinc in 1952 and the success of a miniature of the state coach produced for the Festival of Britain in 1951 that paved the way for one of their biggest successes. Realizing the potential of reissuing their state coach in time for the coronation, Lesney manufactured a gilded version of the tiny horse-drawn vehicle. A million of them were snapped up.

This is a more recent production of the famous Matchbox Gold State Coach, the toy which put the company on the map when it was first produced for the 1953 coronation.

Inspired by War

The year following the coronation, another big media event for the British was the premier of *The Dam Busters*, the World War Two block-buster from 1954 chronicling the heroic activities of Guy Gibson VC's 617 Squadron as they attempted to breach the Ruhr dams with Barnes Wallis's 'bouncing bomb'. Naturally, model kits of Lancaster bombers abounded. British makers FROG and Airfix both had Lancaster bombers in their ranges in the 1950s, though none were of the modified BIII versions as flown by Gibson (Richard Todd in the movie), the 'bouncing bomb' code-named 'UPKEEP' being still on the secrets list!

Interestingly, the Korean War, which lasted from June 1950 until July 1953, and was the first real test of the United Nations, didn't encourage the toy, model or indeed the movie industries to produce product related to that somewhat remote conflict. The Second World War was still bitingly fresh in most people's minds and its campaigns somewhat easier to assimilate. Victory over Japan in August 1945 also neatly brought World War Two to an end. There were clear winners and losers, unlike in Korea where the protagonists had to agree to accept a DMZ (demilitarized zone), which followed more or less the same border that had existed three years before shots were fired.

Although the Korean War highlighted the disharmony between differing cultural, economic and political beliefs, which would come to a head in Vietnam more than ten years later, most Westerners looked to the 1939–45 conflict for all the lessons of courage, suffering and technical wizardry they required.

Similarly, film and TV producers, with publishers and toy manufacturers in train, looked no further than the Battle of Britain, the hunt for German surface raiders, tales of espionage in occupied France and, of course, films dealing with the Allied invasion of Europe for inspiration when considering new productions. The resulting 1950s 'war films', *Angels One Five* (1952), *The Battle of the River Plate* (1956), *The Man Who Never Was* (1956) and *Carve Her Name With Pride* (1958), all bear testimony to a fascination for stories about World War Two which endures to this day.

Featuring wily Sergeant Bilko, *The Phil Silvers Show* was broadcast on US network TV between 1955 and 1959.

This FROG Avro Lancaster was one of the many construction kits of the famous British bomber given a boost in the 1950s following the success of the hit British film, *The Dam Busters*.

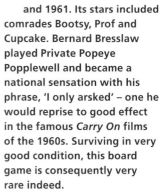

Featuring a bunch of National Servicemen constantly trying to outwit their fiery Sergeant-Major (William Hartnell, a future Doctor Who), *The Army Game* was broadcast between 1957 and 1961. Its stars included comrades Bootsy, Prof and Cupcake. Bernard Bresslaw played Private Popeye Popplewell and became a national sensation with his phrase, 'I only arsked' – one he would reprise to good effect in the famous *Carry On* films of the 1960s. Surviving in very good condition, this board game is consequently very rare indeed.

LEFT: This British-made *Emergency Ward 10* toy features tiny alloy castings of hospital beds, patients and nurses.

The Future Arrives: Dan Dare

No survey of popular British toys of the 1950s can be complete without mentioning one popular media hero, who was neither a star of radio nor of TV – Dan Dare, of course.

Dan Dare was the futuristic star of *Eagle* comic and first appeared on the news stands on 14 April 1950. Drawn by the legendary Frank Hampson, Dan Dare was an instant success.

The launch of publisher Hulton Press's *Eagle* comic was supported by a massive £30,000 advertising campaign and was soon to become an institution with British schoolboys. The weekly comic chronicled Dan Dare and his sidekick Digby's struggle against the evil Mekon, one of the first of numerous malevolent space aliens, which have since become a staple of science fiction.

Such was the success of *Eagle*, and Dan Dare in particular, that manufacturers clamoured for merchandising opportunities. One, the Dorking Foundry, decided that reissuing its existing Vulcan model kit range under the Eagle banner might revitalize its products. Consequently, the Vulcan range was repackaged in stout

RIGHT: **Set in the fictitious Oxbridge General Hospital, Britain's first medical soap opera, *Emergency-Ward 10*, was broadcast from 1957 until 1967.**

BOTTOM: ***Circus Boy* was broadcast in the USA between 1956 and 1958. It starred future Monkees' drummer, Mickey Dolenz, in the title role, although at the time his screen credit was 'Mickey Braddock'.**

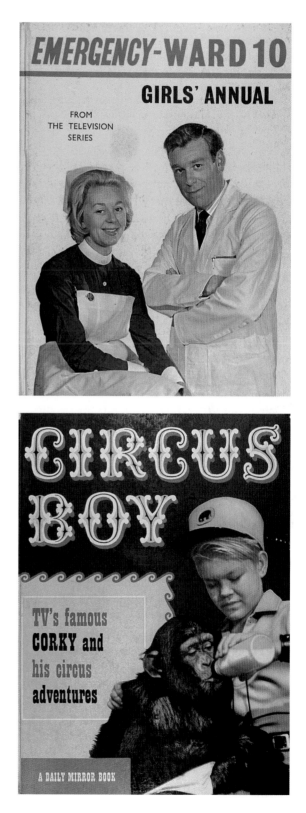

boxes emblazoned with *Eagle*'s masthead and accompanied by full-colour illustrations in *Eagle*'s signature style (the bagged Vulcan range featured simple one-colour headers with dull illustrations and which doubled up as instruction leaflets). The new range was branded 'Eaglewall' and was an immediate success with consumers. The Eaglewall range included the usual 'bankers' like Spitfires, Hurricanes and Me109s, but also an interesting range of World War Two warships depicting incidents from famous naval engagements. These included actions such as the Battle of the River Plate and the famous Altmark incident, when British POWs were plucked off the eponymous German prison ship from the supposed security of a remote Norwegian fjord.

Other more traditional Dan Dare-inspired toys included ray guns, jigsaw puzzles and even a Dan Dare Space Control Radio Station by Merit. This elaborate unit promised to 'send and receive voice and code for up to half a mile'.

The Space Race

The final major 1950s event and one which emphasized the emerging importance of electronics as well as the growing East–West hostility of the deepening Cold War was, of course, the launch of the world's first artificial satellite, *Sputnik*, in October 1957.

Sputnik heralded the start of the Soviet–US space race and the emergence of Khrushchev's technically proficient Communist state. Followed almost immediately by *Sputnik* 2, carrying the first living passenger, a dog called Laika, these inventions seemed for most observers to be straight out of the pages of science fiction. Not surprisingly, the paranoia engendered by

Made between 1959 and 1960, the TV series *Interpol Calling* was based on the cases of the International Criminal Police Organization, based in an office building situated close to the Arc de Triomphe in Paris. The black and white series ran to thirty-nine half-hour episodes and starred Hungarian-born actor Charles Korvin as Inspector Paul Duval.

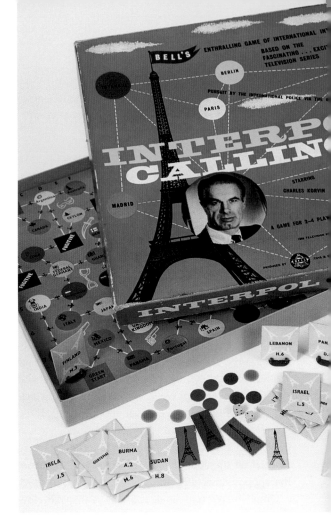

the realization that the Soviets were so far ahead of the affluent Americans spawned dozens of novels and pulp fiction and just as many TV shows and B-movies capitalizing on the fear of the unknown.

Today, most sociologists recognize that films such as *The Day the Earth Stood Still* (1951), *Them!* (1954), *This Island Earth* (1955) and *Forbidden Planet* (1956) symbolize the West's fear of the so-called 'Red Menace' characterized by the rabid anti-Communism of the McCarthy era.

Naturally, toy makers had a field day. Plastic construction kit companies, most notably US ones like Revell and especially Monogram, mirrored youthful interest in rockets, missiles and space stations. Monogram quickly released replicas of America's contributions to the 'space race' and the manufacturer marked all of NASA's milestone inventions through the Gemini, Mercury and Apollo programmes. The company also immortalized many of the weird and wonderful hypothetical designs that abounded at the time, committing them to polystyrene kit form.

At the war's end, most of Germany's World War Two 'V weapon' rocket engineers were spirited away by American intelligence to work for the US military. The most famous of these individuals was V2 designer Werner Von Braun, but a colleague of his, Willy Ley, was probably a more prolific, if fanciful, visionary. Monogram's extensive range of Willy Ley's 'Signature Designs' depict many of his weird and wonderful proposals and have since become enormously collectable.

William Tell was broadcast for only one season in 1958–59. It starred Conrad Phillips in the title role and generated enough interest to warrant its own merchandised items, such as this jigsaw puzzle.

It's fitting that the end of the 1950s should see US toy and model designers fanaticizing about the kinds of space technology that might appear in the future. It wouldn't be long before a new decade would finally see US hegemony in the space race secured in an unprecedented way.

THE 1960s: TOP TV, THE BIG MOVIES, MEDIA EVENTS

With the arrival of the 1960s, modern methods of mass production, most of them designed to support the unprecedented demand for domestic appliances, motor vehicles and entertainment equipment, were rapidly being developed. The 1960s witnessed the dawn of the type of consumerism we all take for granted today. Before this, purchasers of cars and household machinery

expected them to last for years. The 'disposable age' was upon us.

Similarly, up to the 1960s, toys had generally been far more robust than those that were now being produced. Indeed, the new decade can be characterized as the period when, apart from die-cast toy vehicles of course, the majority of toys were manufactured from

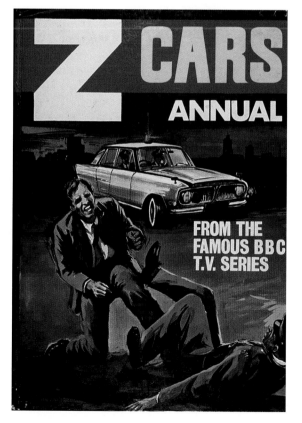

Z Cars had a long and successful run on British TV between 1962 and 1978. One of its stars in the earliest days (1962–65) was a very youthful Brian Blessed.

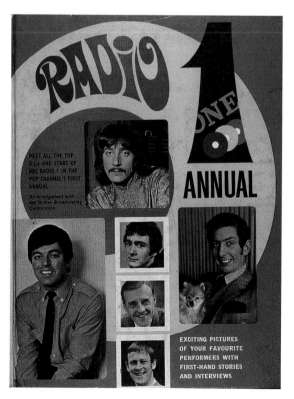

BBC Radio One, a radio station aimed solely at hip young things, went live in 1967. It employed many of the DJs who'd made a living on the North Sea unlicensed 'pirate' stations. This, Radio One's first-ever annual, dates from 1969 and is now quite a rare item.

Belonging to the late Ian Frank Mitchell (in the boater), this World Cup Willie English lion souvenir is a relic of the 1966 World Cup. The photos show Mr Mitchell and gang celebrating England's victory in front of his brand new Morris motor car.

BELOW LEFT: The BBC's *Crackerjack* programme was first broadcast in 1955. Michael Aspel presented it from 1969 until 1973.

BELOW RIGHT: RoSPA, the Royal Society for the Prevention of Accidents, founded the Tufty Club in 1961.

Doctor Kildare starred Richard Chamberlain and was broadcast from 1961–66. Despite its somewhat squashed box, this jigsaw puzzle survives more or less intact.

BELOW LEFT: Children could have fun colouring in pictures from the famous US NBC series in this activity book.

BELOW RIGHT: There are a huge number of 'Corrie' fans out there. Early items associated with the long-running soap (which was first broadcast in 1960) are very rare and much sought after by aficionados. This vintage jigsaw puzzle is one such item.

injection-moulded plastic. The combination of improved and cheaper production techniques and expanding television audiences (although somewhat at the cost of cinema attendances) saw the expansion of several classic toy brands, many of which are still around today.

The decade also saw the emergence of two massively influential figures in the developing story of TV- and film-related toys: James Bond and Gerry Anderson. More about these two heroes – one fictional and one real – later.

The High Point of TV Westerns

Although its genesis was in 1959, *Rawhide*, the enormously popular TV cowboy series that featured none other than Clint Eastwood as Rowdy Yates, ran for 217 sixty-minute episodes until 1966. Indeed, Clint Eastwood was hired by the Italian 'spaghetti Western' director Sergio Leone for a knockdown price of $15,000 to star in *A Fistful of Dollars, For a Few Dollars More* and *The Good, The Bad and the Ugly* whilst he was still recording *Rawhide*.

LEFT: **TV Westerns were ever-popular.** *Laramie* **was broadcast between 1959 and 1963.**

BELOW LEFT: *Wagon Train* **was broadcast in colour on American TV between 1962–65.**

BELOW RIGHT: *Gunsmoke* **starred James Arness and was broadcast from 1959 until 1961.**

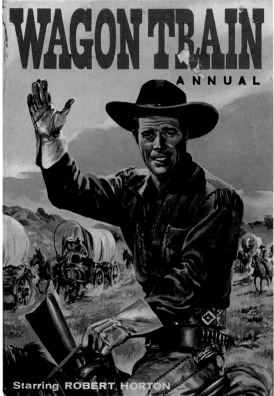

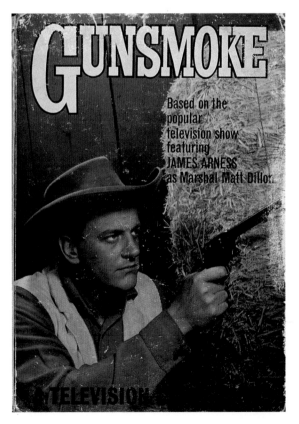

Bonanza was first on our screens in 1959. Incredibly, the show continued in production until 1973. This annual is from the 1960s.

Broadcast from 1959 until 1966, *Rawhide* was the TV series that launched Clint Eastwood's career, drawing him to the attention of Italian 'spaghetti Western' director Sergio Leone. The rest is history.

Westerns were a perennial favourite of the 1960s and whilst series like *Rawhide* mostly generated spin-off merchandise only in the form of books and annuals, other programmes within the genre, notably *Bonanza* (1959–73) and *The High Chaparral* (1967–71), were catalyst to a whole range of toys from cap-firing revolvers and one-third scale Winchester repeaters, to stetsons and numerous alloy 'sheriff's badges'. Buck, Billy Blue, Big John, Manolito and the lovely Victoria from Arizona's High Chaparral ranch were even immortalized in a set of Airfix HO-OO scale polythene figures.

Although produced to a much higher standard than was previously the case, with scripts written by a new wave of young talent, many of whom were going to make their mark in a big way a decade later, there were some programmes that took liberties with familiar subjects.

Within the Western genre, *F-Troop* (1965–67) poked fun at some of the almost venerated precepts of the group. Cavalry Captain Wilton Parmenter becomes a hero by accidentally leading a cavalry charge the wrong way and is given command of the remote outpost of Fort Courage for his sins. Despite featuring Hollywood staples like Forrest Tucker, who played Sgt Morgan O'Rourke, *F-Troop* broke the mould. It was definitely not in the John Ford tradition; perhaps because of this, but especially because of its slapstick humour, kids loved it.

Another startlingly original TV Western series was *Branded* (1965–66). The show ran for thirty-two episodes, filmed in colour, and starred Chuck Connors as ex-West Point graduate Captain Jason McCord. McCord, the only survivor from an Indian massacre at the Battle of Bitter Creek, was assumed to have fled the scene of combat as a coward. Consequently, the US army top brass wanted him 'branded' as such. His sword famously snapped in front of him, McCord leaves the army in disgrace and the series follows his various stirring exploits as he strives to clear his name.

A Different Take on the War

The rawness of the war years had somewhat mellowed by the 1960s. Producers felt they could be freer with their treatment of certain traditional themes that had previously been sacrosanct. *Hogan's Heroes* (1965–71)

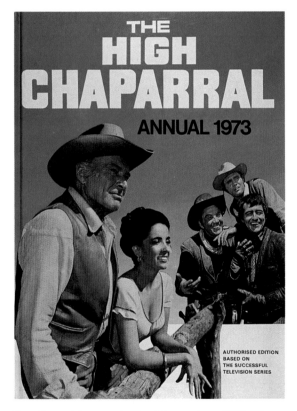

Together with annuals like this one from 1973, *The High Chaparral* (1967–71) was catalyst to a whole range of toys, from cap-firing revolvers and 1/3 scale Winchester repeaters, to stetsons and numerous alloy sheriff's badges. Buck, Billy Blue, Big John, Manolito and the lovely Victoria from Arizona's High Chaparral ranch were immortalized in a set of Airfix HO-OO scale polythene figures.

was one such programme, based on a familiar theme – bad Germans, good Allies – but treated not with the traditional victor's self-righteousness that characterized so many stories recalling World War Two, but with humour.

Set in a German POW camp, the series ran to 168 episodes and followed the exploits of American Col Robert E. Hogan (played by Bob Crane) and his fellow inmates as they tried to outwit Nazi camp commandant Col Klink and the hapless Sgt Schultz. Despite making a laugh out of a regime that was in reality a very severe system, the progamme went some way in ameliorating the not-uncommon view that all Nazis had to be cold-blooded killers. The fat Sgt Schultz was particularly popular with children and his face graced comics and annuals when the series was broadcast. Action figure manufacturer Sideshow Collectibles even released 12in toy dolls of Schultz, Hogan and other characters from the series as recently as the late 1990s, further proof of the programme's enduring popularity.

Despite the fact that the majority of 1960s films and TV series were still based on familiar lines, there was a new honesty to the productions. No longer were 'goodies and baddies' as clearly defined as before. The heroes might still have worn the white hats but producers and script writers, free of Senator McCarthy's accusations of being closet Soviet agents, were at last able to touch on aspects dealing with inequities like racism and misogyny. Indeed, *The High Chaparral* was one of the first Westerns to portray Native Americans – Apaches – as people, not mindless savages.

Star Trek Begins

As all true fans of 1960s and 1970s TV shows – and especially the ones that have endured partly through toy merchandising – know, the most influential TV show of this period, especially regarding interracial relationships, was also one of the most innovative in purely creative ways. Gene Rodenberry's *Star Trek*, on television more or less continually since 1966, is in the same league as 007 and *Star Wars* when it comes to successful franchising. Amazingly, on Friday, 8 September 2006, *Star Trek* celebrated the fortieth anniversary of its first broadcast!

An alien form invades the Enterprise through Spock's mind!

AN ALIEN FORM INVADES THE ENTERPRISE THROUGH SPOCK'S MIND!

Early (1969) edition of a *Star Trek* comic by US publisher Gold Key.

The Creations of Gerry Anderson

Let's start by looking at the career of *Thunderbirds*' creator, Gerry Anderson. Although some of his new ideas took off in the mid to late 1950s, he really hit the big time in the 1960s as the story of his prodigious output, shown below, testifies.

After discovering that an allergy to building plaster probably meant that a career as a professional architect was a non-starter, Gerry Anderson joined the British film industry as a trainee. In 1946, his name first appeared on production titles when he was appointed assistant director on the Gainsborough Films production of *Caravan*, a period piece starring Stewart Granger.

After National Service, in 1949 Anderson went to London's Pinewood Studios and resumed his production career as a dubbing editor. Following a five-year stint behind the scenes, he took the bold step of founding his own commercials company, Pentagon Films. However, commissions for Pentagon and its more famous descendant, AP Films, were few and far between.

Fortunately, in 1955 an approach from the independent television pioneer, Associated Rediffusion, resulted in a commission for a new puppet series, *The Adventures of Twizzle*. Little did Anderson know it then, but this programme and its follow-up, *Torchy the Battery Boy*, were about to cement a relationship between Gerry Anderson and SFX puppetry which would lead to numerous classic children's TV shows.

Following *The Adventures of Twizzle*, Anderson decided to produce his own puppet shows. The first of these was *Four Feather Falls*, which was underwritten by Granada Television. About this time, Anderson also came to the attention of legendary television impresario Lew Grade, then head of the giant ATV organization.

With Grade's money behind him, Anderson was able to consider even more sophisticated productions, pioneering many revolutionary techniques and ultimately establishing his own unique 'Supermarionation' process. Years before George Lucas's lucrative

Despite *Star Trek* being a huge hit almost immediately, only American kit manufacturer AMT really jumped on the bandwagon when the show débuted, releasing a kit of the USS *Enterprise* in 1966. It wasn't until the early 1970s that merchandised products, other than the 'usual suspects' of annuals, comics and novellas, really took off.

The Brits could cut the mustard too as far as science fiction was concerned. Although working, initially at least, with a budget somewhat smaller than that of *Star Trek*, a small cadre of British visionaries captured their own view of the future, creating new worlds and populating them with aliens and fantastic machines that thrilled TV audiences every week. They still do.

The programmes? *Thunderbirds* and the many other Gerry Anderson creations and, of course, *Doctor Who*. *Thunderbirds* enjoyed rather more freedom than the chronicles of the ever-regenerating Time Lord, including at one time the not inconsiderable financial support of Independent Television's Lew Grade. *Doctor Who* had to work to somewhat tighter budgets, being a product of the publicly funded British Broadcasting Corporation.

Star Wars merchandise deal, Anderson had grasped the significance of third-party merchandise contracts. He quickly established the Century 21 Organisation, which marketed a vast range of monthly comics and annual periodicals centred on Anderson's growing portfolio of science fiction and fantasy productions. Shrewdly, Century 21 only granted toy licences to the best manufacturers, ensuring that toys related to the shows were of a quality equivalent to the high production values Anderson demanded of his TV shows.

Consequently, the myriad Dinky toys and Airfix models licensed by Century 21 are of top quality and command the very highest prices on the collectors' market.

Gerry Anderson's prodigious career is full of highlights. A glance at the shows he produced during the 1960s is dizzying. The TV series are detailed below, but there were motion films too.

AP Films, the forerunner of his legendary Century 21 Organisation, produced *Supercar*, the real taster of things to come from Anderson's fertile brain. First broadcast during the1960–61 season, twenty-six twenty-five-minute episodes were produced. They followed the adventures of test pilot Mike Mercury and his fantastic vehicle, Supercar, which could operate on land, sea and in the air.

Today, one of the most coveted vintage *Supercar* collectables is British manufacturer Budgie's replica of Mike Mercury's incredible vehicle. The Budgie miniature was painted in Supercar's striking red and silver colour

scheme and featured a figure of Mike Mercury, moveable wings and rolling wheels for added play value.

Such was the popularity of *Supercar* on the other side of the Atlantic that US manufacturers, notably Remco Industries of Harrison, New Jersey, also snapped up a

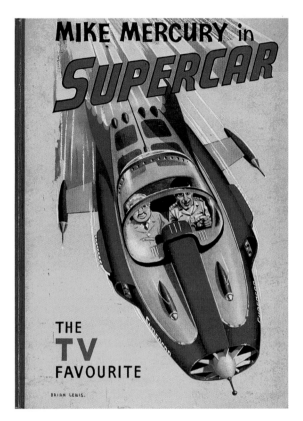

Rare *Supercar* annual from 1961.

A BRIEF HISTORY OF DINKY TOYS

The legendary Dinky brand began life in 1933 as 'Modelled Miniatures', part of Frank Hornby's enormous toy empire. The name was changed to Dinky in 1934. Dinkies were manufactured in two plants – Binns Road in Liverpool and Bobigny in France. In 1963 the British arm of Dinky was purchased by Tri-ang. French Dinky carried on autonomously.

Much to the consternation of die-hard collectors who demanded that Dinky should only release accurate replicas of automobiles and commercial vehicles, by the late 1960s the Binns Road plant began producing replicas of fantasy creations from popular TV series and films. Consequently, a range of themed releases based on Gerry Anderson programmes like *Thunderbirds* and *Captain Scarlet* and die-cast miniatures of *Star Trek* space ships were added to the range.

Rare British-made Fireball XL5 game of Snap. Bought in the 1960s by Steve Zodiac fan, Nigel Gray.

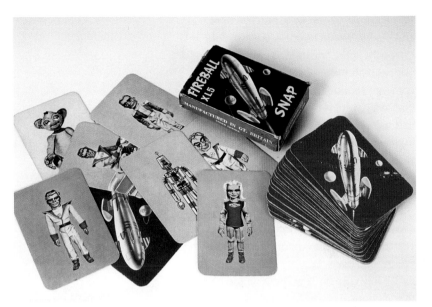

BELOW: This early annual from Gerry Anderson's next production, *Fireball XL5*, is highly sought after by Anderson fans.

manufacturing licence. That company's replica was larger and somewhat more elaborate than the Budgie release. Part of *Supercar*'s popularity stateside was, of course, the fact that the advanced vehicle was housed in a secret base in the Nevada Desert. In 1963, Remco also manufactured a flying model of Supercar. It could be launched and made to perform a variety of manoeuvres.

Other popular *Supercar* toys from the 1960s included lunch boxes and thermos flasks, 'sweet cigarette' cards, alarm clocks and money boxes (one by manufacturer Linda combining both functions) and the inevitable array of comic book articles and annuals dedicated to the programme. However, my favourites include British manufacturer Merit's 'Supercar Intercom Set' and a Milton Bradley (MB) board game dating from 1962, 'Supercar to the Rescue'.

Gerry Anderson's next production, *Fireball XL5*, was even more successful than its predecessor. Produced between 1962–63, thirty-nine half-hour episodes were made. Relating the exploits of a 300ft rocket-powered space ship, piloted by Col Steve Zodiac, *Fireball XL5* was in tune with the zeitgeist of the times – the East–West race for victory in space.

Fireball XL5 also had the advantage of having more rounded characters in its script than *Supercar* did, as well as benefiting from the humour derived from the antics of Robert the Robot and Zoonie, a loveable space monkey of the alien species, the Lazoons.

Not surprisingly, *Fireball XL5* toys were produced in equal profusion to those manufactured for *Supercar*.

Those surviving today, especially mint and boxed Pelham puppets, are especially sought after. Incidentally, the British puppet manufacturer Pelham, the famous company founded in 1947 by Bob Pelham that sadly went into receivership in 1992, had a long history of producing puppets licensed from most of Gerry Anderson's shows. This is perhaps not so surprising, bearing in mind that many of Anderson's shows were ... based on puppets!

In 1963 Anderson's AP Films made *Stingray*, another Supermarionation series. Set in the year 2065, the fearless personnel of WASP (the World Aquanaut Security Patrol), but most noticeably Captain Troy Tempest and his communications expert Phones in their fantastic nuclear-powered submarine *Stingray*, battle against the evil Aquaphibians, led by their ruler Titan. From their base at Marineville HQ, *Stingray* fights to prevent the Aquaphibians from invading the surface world in revenge for the recent marine exploration activities of the landlubbers. Troy and Phones are aided in the fight by the lovely but mute mermaid Marina and a shore team comprising of Atlanta, who burns a candle for Troy, and her father, Commander Sam Shore, the boss of WASP. 'Anything Can Happen in the Next Half-Hour' was the programme's catchphrase – and it usually did.

Two distinct themes recur in Anderson's work. Firstly, the protagonists are usually either a security force or rescue service, and secondly the aliens are generally provoked to violence following the benevolent but naïve activities of humans. The almost UN-like charter of *Thunderbirds* International Rescue to save those in distress and Captain Black's unwitting attack on a Martian base provoking the wrath of the Mysterons in *Captain Scarlet* spring to mind.

Whilst there were a few toys of the actual *Stingray* submarine produced at the time the series was broadcast, ironically more and better representations of the supersubmarine have been produced in recent years. However, one manufacturer producing replicas of the supersub contemporarily with *Stingray*'s original TV broadcast was British manufacturer Lincoln International. In 1963,

Stingray Annual from 1965.

the company produced a lovely plastic *Stingray* replica. The box, predominately coloured in sea-green, featured a view of the silver, yellow and blue vessel diving to the murky ocean depths.

Two manufacturers of note, which produce excellent replicas of *Stingray* today, in a variety of scales, are Johnny Lightning and Product Enterprises. One of the reasons for the omission of quality toys from the early 1960s is that until the enormous success of *Thunderbirds*, which made the leap from television to cinema and encouraged Gerry Anderson to establish Century 21 and at last retain the merchandising rights for his new series, he had little control over what was produced. However, amongst the many toys emanating from the

RIGHT: 'Under the oceans of the world, the deadly super-sub STINGRAY cruises silently, pitting its lightning speed and efficiency against the evil Titan and his race of Aquaphibians.'

BELOW: *Stingray: The Deadly Alliance* annual from 1966.

series, which ran to thirty-nine twenty-five minute episodes, was a toy gun manufactured in green and red painted alloy by the British firm, Lone Star. Interestingly, although the box featured stirring artwork showing the implacable Troy Tempest brandishing the weapon, it was in fact identical to the Dan Dare ray gun that Lone Star had produced a decade earlier. Incidentally, Lone Star was so named because of the popularity of Westerns with children of the 1950s.

As every toy collector knows, the top-quality Gerry Anderson-related items really began with *Thunderbirds*. The original thirty-two fifty-minute episodes were originally broadcast between 1964 and 1966; they have been repeated many, many times since.

By the mid-1960s, Anderson and his team – wife Sylvia, associate producer Reg Hill, art director Bob Bell and SFX director Derek Meddings – were so successful that Anderson could insist on only the best representations of his creations. It is therefore no surprise that Dinky Toys, one of the biggest and certainly most famous die-cast toy manufacturers in the world,

ABOVE LEFT: *Thunderbirds* annual *1968*.

ABOVE RIGHT: 'For Girls Who Love Television', the *Lady Penelope Annual* 1967.

RIGHT: 'The City of Darkness', one of the many stories featuring Lady Penelope, devoured by young girls in the 1960s.

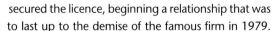

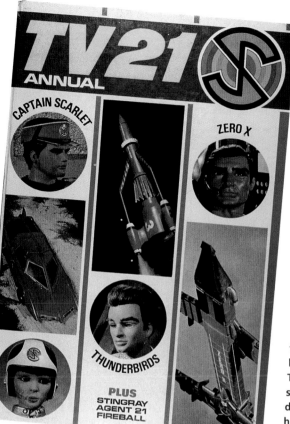

secured the licence, beginning a relationship that was to last up to the demise of the famous firm in 1979.

In 1967, against stiff competition especially from British rival Corgi, which up until then had usually been awarded the merchandising rights to film and TV product, Dinky Toys won the concession to produce Gerry Anderson's *Thunderbirds*-related products. Although

'Adventure in the 21st Century. It is 2067. Man is master of the universe. From the sprawling capitals of the Earth vast space liners drift across the blackness of space, linking the planets and asteroids of the Earth Space Empire. It is a time of scientific advancement, of change and discovery. It is a time, too, of danger and excitement.' Fortunately, on the pages of the wonderful *TV21* annuals youngsters were reassured that the world was in the safe hands of organizations like International Rescue, which, with its fleet of Thunderbirds rockets and vehicles, would make sure everything was 'FAB'. These three *TV21 Annuals* date from the 1960s and are becoming increasingly hard to find.

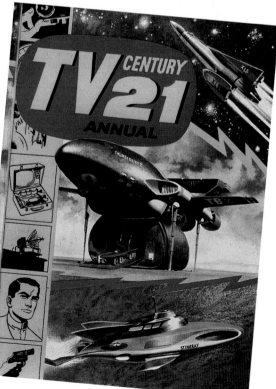

Anderson's own TV 21 Organisation licensed *Thunderbirds* products to other manufacturers such as Lincoln Inc. of America and a Hong Kong-based manufacturer, Rosenthal, it is the Dinky replicas of Thunderbird 2 and Lady Penelope's spectacular pink Rolls Royce that have endured.

The Dinky Toys' Thunderbird 2 die-cast 'Straight from *Thunderbirds*', as it says on the box, was a revelation.

Finished in the authentic green colouring of the TV vehicle and with spring-operated extending legs and a detachable pod containing a highly accurate miniature of the aquatic Thunderbird 4, it sold by the million. Original boxed versions of this die-cast are worth hundreds of pounds. The toy was re-released by Dinky in 1973, but, curiously, this version, presented in a blister pack rather than the much more attractive box, for

Lovely *Thunderbirds* water pistol, a Junior TV21 product from the late 1960s.

BELOW: **Extremely rare and very collectable Lincoln snap-together construction kit of Lady Penelope's FAB 1 car from Gerry Anderson's ground-breaking *Thunderbirds*. This kit even featured an electric motor. It dates from 1966.**

This *Thunderbirds* 3-D painting-by-numbers set enabled children to complete a dramatic scene from the hit show.

some inexplicable reason was coloured a metallic blue. Though manufactured from the same tools as the 1967 version and possessing the same operating features, this later variant is worth considerably less.

The Dinky Lady Penelope's FAB 1 was also originally available in a box, but from around 1970 onwards was repackaged in a blister pack. As with Thunderbirds 2, the earlier versions of this toy command the highest prices. FAB 1 also featured firing rockets. These are easily lost and although repro versions are available, die-casts complete with the original missiles are worth the highest amounts.

Other *Thunderbirds* products of note include a series of dolls representing characters from the show, produced by Fairylite in the 1960s, and painting-by-numbers sets (there was even a 3-D approach available from Rosenthal Toys), and a 'Thunderbirds to the Rescue Marble Maze' manufactured by Peter Pan Playthings, which required youngsters to gently shake ball-bearings into the correct holes en route to a rendezvous at a rescue scene.

Captain Scarlet and the Mysterons was Gerry Anderson's next big thing. Broadcast in 1967 and comprising thirty-two twenty-five minute episodes, the series followed the exploits of SPECTRUM's indestructible Captain Scarlet as he battled with the Mysterons, an alien race intent on world domination aided and abetted by the dastardly double agent, Captain Black.

Captain Scarlet featured some of Century 21's most imaginative designs yet. There was a variety of vehicles, a kind of flying aircraft carrier called Cloudbase from which interceptor jet fighters all piloted by women – the Angels – could be launched in support of SPECTRUM.

Gerry Anderson's Century 21 organization enabled him to at last retain the merchandising rights for all his new productions. Along with comics and annuals, Century 21 branched out into toys, as can be seen by this rare mint and boxed battery-operated Mobile Bridge & Combat Tank dating from 1968.

The success of the various licence arrangements in support of *Thunderbirds* had finally convinced manufacturers that had been unwilling or unable to reach an agreement with Century 21 to secure concessions. One of these firms was the famous south London plastic construction kit manufacturer, Airfix, which in 1968 released a 1/72 scale plastic kit of an Angel interceptor. Although this model has been regularly re-released, examples in the original box are worth several hundred pounds.

Fresh from its enormous success with *Thunderbirds*, Dinky was keen to secure the concession for *Captain Scarlet* die-casts as well. The resulting Dinky *Captain Scarlet* die-cast vehicles are arguably some of the best and certainly most collectable the famous brand ever manufactured.

As fans of Gerry Anderson and of *Captain Scarlet* in particular know, SPECTRUM's vehicles were some of the most imaginative and aesthetically pleasing ever produced. Beginning with Captain Scarlet's shark-nosed red SPC (Spectrum Patrol Car) released in 1968 and in full production until 1975, these were the Dinky Toys every boy wanted.

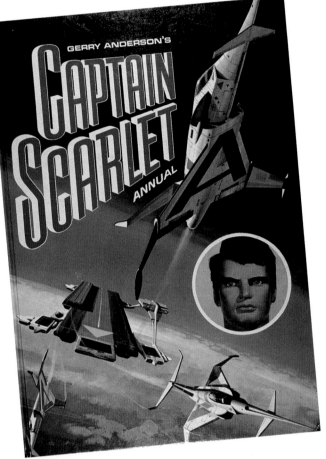

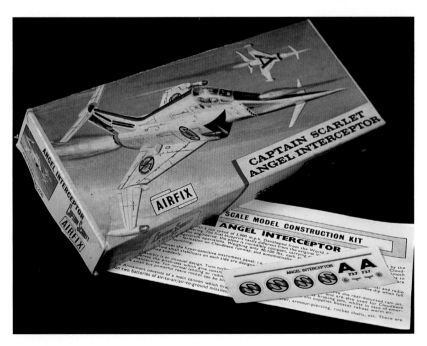

ABOVE: *Gerry Anderson's Captain Scarlet Annual* from 1967 and published by Century 21 Publishing Ltd. Inside it says: 'Captain Scarlet is indestructible – you are not. Remember this and do not try to imitate him.'

LEFT: 1968 original issue of the Airfix 1/72 scale kit of an Angel Interceptor.

**Mint and boxed Spectrum
Patrol Car (SPC); Dinky, 1968.**

The SPC was the cheapest of the trio of *Captain Scarlet* die-casts. Next in line was the MSV (Maximum Security Vehicle). The armoured SPC's purpose was to transport VIPs securely and to carry valuable cargoes. This white and red vehicle was an object lesson in streamlining. It featured neat gull-wing doors and inside a crate of 'radioactive' material could be found. Collectors should note that this crate was easily lost, so its presence is a premium. Another thing to note is that in general the vehicle's interior was red. Some production batches featured blue interiors and as is

the same with short-run colour variants on other die-casts, this anomaly is of most value.

The daddy of them all, as far as *Captain Scarlet* vehicles are concerned, is the large metallic blue SPV (Spectrum Pursuit Vehicle). This toy replicates all the features of the vehicle from the TV programme: Captain Scarlet himself could be released seated, backwards, in a seat that slid out from a side door; rear-mounted Caterpillar tracks could be engaged to provide extra traction; and a press of one of the antennae fairings on the roof would open a hatch in the nose and fire a deadly missile!

**Wonderful Dinky Spectrum
Pursuit Vehicle (SPV) from
1968. Captain Scarlet can be
seen sitting in his rear-facing
chair. This was a 'real' toy, the
author's own. It is without its
box and shows evidence of
having been involved in some
pretty vigorous adventures.**

Obviously, boxed examples of this toy are worth top dollar. However, such is its nostalgic appeal, even to non-toy collectors, that most men who grew up during the 1960s and 1970s still covet ownership of an SPV. One of the reasons is simply that when it was originally released it was a relatively expensive toy and not a parental impulse purchase like so many other die-cast vehicles were.

Surviving examples of the SPV are worth money in almost any condition. Things to look out for, however, are: operating mechanisms (the side door and the nose-mounted hatch often being damaged); the presence of Captain Scarlet himself of course; rubber tracks; and the most commonly missing piece – the rubber-tipped missile. It's worth pointing out, though, that there are

ABOVE LEFT: **Rare Century 21 *Captain Scarlet Painting Book* from 1968.**

BELOW LEFT AND RIGHT: **Before 'Charlie's Angels' there were 'Gerry's Angels': Destiny, Harmony, Rhapsody, Symphony and Melody.**

scores of small manufacturers that service the collectors' market and make replacement parts of almost all of the items that might be missing.

Other *Captain Scarlet* collectables include Pelham puppets, Timpo 2in (54mm) figures of the Captain, plus a super 12in (305mm) Captain Scarlet doll and a 3in (76mm) bendy miniature of Destiny Angel (there were five pilots in all, of differing nationalities, the others being Harmony, Rhapsody, Symphony and Melody), both manufactured in Britain by Pedigree Toys. In addition, there were, of course, countless annuals, colouring books, mugs, beakers and stationery accessories.

Joe 90 was Gerry Anderson's next foray. It was produced between 1967–68 and ran to some thirty twenty-five-minute episodes. Nowhere near as popular with

RIGHT: **Timpo toy figure of Captain Scarlet (54mm scale), 1969.**

BELOW LEFT and RIGHT: **Gerry Anderson's *Joe 90* was produced between 1967–68. These annuals date from the period.**

kids as *Captain Scarlet*, nevertheless it had enough clout to attract a variety of manufacturers to bid for concession opportunities.

Naturally, Dinky Toys was at the front of the queue. Its offering was a superb rendition of Joe's car, the multifaceted jet-powered vehicle that emerged from concealment in a half-timbered cottage. Dinky's vehicle featured retractable wings (as you'd expect, this car could fly), while a small bulb powered by a concealed 1.5V battery enabled the engine's exhaust to

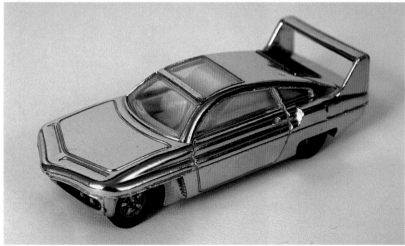

ABOVE LEFT: **Gerry Anderson's** *Joe 90* **was produced between 1967–68. This annual dates from the period.**

ABOVE RIGHT: **This Dinky Toy catalogue dates from May 1969. On the cover, Joe's Car (Dinky No. 102) takes pride of place.**

LEFT: **Sam's car, which came with a keyless clockwork motor, was the other** *Joe 90* **vehicle produced by Dinky.**

flash. In keeping with many other Dinky vehicles produced towards the end of the 1960s, Joe's car was originally available in a cardboard box, then later in a striking blister pack. Rarer variants have red turbines as opposed to the more usual silver-plated versions.

Sam's car, which came with a keyless clockwork motor, was the other *Joe 90* vehicle produced by Dinky. By pushing down on the toy, dragging it backwards and letting it go, you could guarantee that after it had damaged the skirting-board paintwork, your pets would never bother you again.

The box depicted the car in a red finish. However, as the box said, 'colour of model might differ from illustration' and purchasers had a good chance of taking home a silver variant or one in blue, white or even gold. What every purchaser got, though, was a self-adhesive version of Joe's WIN (World Intelligence Network) badge.

As mentioned above, British manufacturer Pedigree had previously obtained the licence for dolls, or what are more properly and manfully called 'action figures' today. The success of the *Captain Scarlet* offerings, especially the 12in (305mm) version of Captain Scarlet, which I recall even featured a flip-down microphone attached to the visor of his cap, encouraged the firm to produce tie-ins in association with *Joe 90*.

Consequently, Pedigree produced an approximately 6in (153mm) tall Joe 90 doll which proved very popular. It even came with a WIN badge and a separate pair of Joe's distinctive glasses.

As with *Captain Scarlet* and *Thunderbirds* before, manufacturers of breakfast cereal, especially Kellogg's, incorporated on-pack promotions linked to *Joe 90*. Particularly collectable are the set of six badges, one of each coming free at random in a packet of *Sugar Smacks*. Ice-cream manufacturer Lyons Maid also produced a cool *Joe 90* badge that was available free in return for five tokens cut from the wrappers of Zoom lollies.

Gerry Anderson's last big show of the 1960s was *UFO*. Anderson's previous successes guaranteed even bigger budgets for new projects. *UFO* was produced on the biggest scale so far and featured real actors for the first time. During the 1969–70 period, twenty-six lavish fifty-minute episodes of this spectacular series were produced. Although Thunderbird 2 is my all-time favourite design from the Gerry Anderson stable, I have to admit that the *UFO* vehicles produced by Dinky especially are probably some of the best toys of the time.

Set in the near future, the early 1980s, *UFO* chronicles the activities of SHADO (Supreme Headquarters Alien Defence Organisation), established to ward off the

A Waddington's jigsaw puzzle showing Joe's car emerging from its rural hideaway.

threat from Aliens who are invading Earth and kid-napping humans for nefarious reasons.

Covertly based in a film studio in London and with a base on the Moon and in possession of a fleet of *Sky-diver* submarines and an orbiting satellite SID (Space Intruder Detector), SHADO was commanded by Commander Ed Straker. Straker could deploy a range of vehicles in his efforts to combat the alien intruders. Principal amongst these was the Alien Interceptor and the SHADO 2 mobile. Both of these vehicles were produced by Dinky Toys and are now very collectable indeed.

Fans have often wondered just how potent the Interceptors would have been in reality. They were armed with only one huge nose-mounted rocket-propelled missile. After this had been fired, they became sterile. One wonders if someone had overlooked this rather grievous tactical error…. The SHADO mobile was a chunky green tracked vehicle that also fired missiles. A flick of a button would cause the roof to revolve, revealing an armed rocket launcher. At least we assumed this vehicle contained a magazine load of extra missiles inside and was therefore capable of continuous fire!

LEFT: Rocket-firing SHADO Mobile 2 from *UFO*. **This vehicle operated on the surface and was intended to take care of any aliens who had evaded the 'one-shot wonders' that were the Interceptors (probably quite a few then). This Dinky Toy (No. 353) was available in green as shown here but also in blue. There were far fewer blue die-casts produced and consequently they are worth significantly more than the green versions.**

Dinky Toys No. 351, the U.F.O. Interceptor, complete with its one missile. Keen-eyed readers will notice that this is a renovated example of the classic Dinky toy and is complete with a repro box. Because of the scarcity and consequent expense of mint and boxed original items, the trade in such 'tidied-up' items is brisk.

RIGHT: **British manufacturer Arrow Games produced this UFO jigsaw puzzle in the early 1970s. It is chock-a-block with many of the marvellous vehicles that kept youngsters glued to TV screens in the early 1970s.**

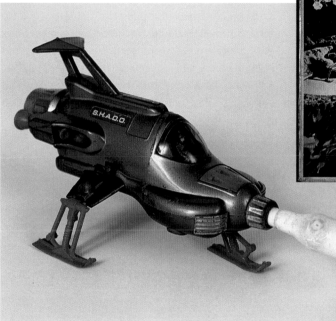

LEFT: **Close-up of an original, locked and loaded Dinky Toys S.H.A.D.O. Interceptor.**

Because they were so substantial, both the above toys survive in fairly large numbers. Interceptors possessing their original missile, or one without a partially perished rubber nose cone, are rare. Boxed examples are even rarer. The Mobile 2 was prone to losing its missile too and occasionally shedding one of its Caterpillar tracks. Other *UFO* toys of note include a set of very rare GAF Viewmaster discs manufactured in 1969, a set of collectable sweet cigarette cards from British manufacturer Bassett's and good examples of *UFO* annuals.

Doctor Who Starts His Travels

No review of 1960s British science-fiction toys and products is anywhere near complete, of course, without mention of *Doctor Who*, the BBC TV series that has been an institution with fans for more than forty years

and is as much of a cult amongst enthusiasts as are *Star Trek* and *Star Wars*.

On the evening of 23 November 1963, British audiences first heard the distinctive synthesized tones of Ron Grainer's classic theme as interpreted by the BBC's Radiophonic Workshop. *Doctor Who* was born.

The brainchild of the BBC Head of Drama, Sydney Newman, and others in the BBC, including Donald Wilson, 'Bunny' Webber, Anthony Coburn, David Whitaker, the creator of the Daleks, the late Terry Nation, Raymond Cusick and producer Verity Lambert, the programme opened with the first Doctor being played by William Hartnell. The famous time traveller, indeed Time Lord, has regenerated many times since and the tenth Doctor is played by actor David Tennant.

During the programme's long history, the Doctor has faced many malevolent aliens. These have included Ice Warriors, Yetis, Silurians and Cybermen. However, the most famous and enduring are, of course, the Daleks.

Legend has it that Terry Nation thought them up whilst sitting in the BBC canteen wondering how to create a truly original robot (traditionally they had too obviously been actors in silvery rubber suits) within the paltry budget allocated by the public broadcasting corporation. Whilst toying with one of those old-fashioned glass and plastic-topped salt and pepper pots he had his 'eureka'! moment. Another legend is that the Dalek's multi-functional sucker arm was based on a sink plunger that was readily sourced from the BBC's sanitation stores. What's certain is that, originally, these all-conquering armoured mutants from the planet Skaro could be defeated by… a flight of stairs. Today they have the power to levitate, so no one's safe.

The Daleks were an immediate hit with audiences young and old when they first appeared in December 1963. *The Dalek Book*, which effectively became the first Dalek annual, hit the shops in 1964 and has since become a prized possession amongst collectors. Soon afterwards, manufacturer Louis Marx produced a battery-operated Dalek and this has again become a favourite and very rare collectable. Surviving 1960s toy merchandise is very hard to come by – generally most of the *Doctor Who* toys

Published in 1964, *The Dalek Book* is effectively the first Dr Who annual. It features stunning artwork by illustrator Richard Jennings, who later worked on the seminal *TV21* comics and annuals. This book is naturally cherished by Doctor Who collectors and is rare in any condition.

and action figures that can be found were manufactured in the 1970s and consequently are the subject of the next chapter.

Before we turn to some more 1960s American TV shows that generated a range of supporting toys and games, let's take a brief look at some more British classics from that decade.

Postgate and Firmin's Smallfilms Productions

In the late 1950s, Oliver Postgate was a stage manager at the British TV company Associated Rediffusion and was used to working with a range of inventive stage and production props and techniques to help convey the messages within individual programmes. Deciding that children's television material was what he called 'pretty thin stuff', he chose to create his own programmes. Teaming up with illustrator Peter Firmin, the duo began to fashion programmes in their unique style.

The first really successful Postgate and Firmin Smallfilms Productions were *Ivor the Engine* (ITV, 1959) and the six-part saga of *Noggin the Nog* (BBC, 1959). In the mid-1960s, Smallfilms began its long association with the BBC's *Watch With Mother*, which led to a big success with *Pogles' Wood*.

However, Postgate and Firmin's *Clangers*, their first colour production, is probably their best-remembered

BELOW LEFT: *The Herbs* **was first broadcast in 1968.**

BELOW RIGHT: *Hector's House Annual* **from 1968.**

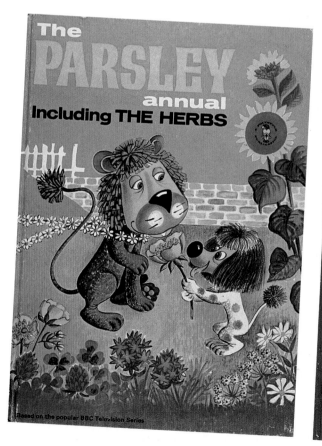

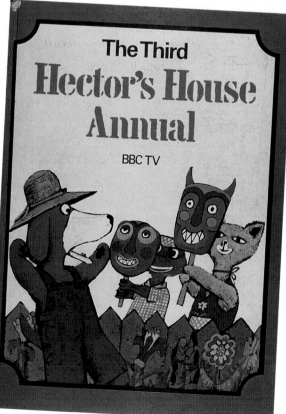

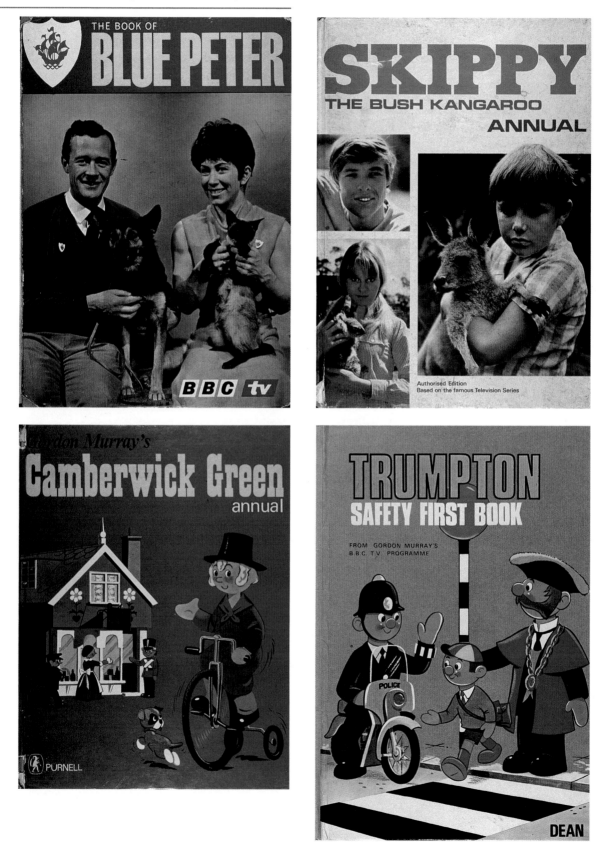

OPPOSITE PAGE:

TOP LEFT: **Featuring Valerie Singleton and Christopher Trace on the front cover,** *The Book of Blue Peter* **was published in 1965. It is the first edition in a long series of** *Blue Peter Annuals* **and is consequently a collectors' item.**

TOP RIGHT: *Skippy*, **the tale of the resourceful bush kangaroo, was a very popular children's programme. Australian-made, it was first broadcast between 1966–68.**

BOTTOM LEFT: Gordon Murray's *Camberwick Green* **was first seen on BBC TV in 1966.**

BOTTOM RIGHT: The BBC's *Trumpton* **was first broadcast in 1967. This** *Safety First Book* **was published in 1969.**

THIS PAGE:
A French hit originally, *The Magic Roundabout* **was first seen on British screens in 1965.**

THE MAGIC ROUNDABOUT
A DAY WITH DOUGAL
based on the popular BBC-TV series
DEAN

On BBC Television between 1969 and 1972, *The Clangers* spawned countless books and soft toy replicas of the friendly pink aliens who spoke only in whistles.

series (although *Bagpuss* comes a close second). *Clangers*, screened on BBC between 1969–72, spawned countless books and soft toy replicas of the friendly pink aliens who spoke only in whistles. Nourished by the 'Blue String Pudding' and 'Green Soup' that the Soup Dragon harvested from the home planet's soup wells, the Clangers lived in craters and were protected from meteor strikes by the dustbin lids they used as doors to shut themselves within. Their name is derived from the sound of impacts upon these metal lids.

Pinky and Perky

Twin boy pigs Pinky and Perky first performed as part of a TV programme called *It's Up to You* in the late 1950s. Created by Jan and Vlasta Dalibar, Czechoslovakian émigrés who had settled in Yorkshire after the war, Pinky and Perky's real career took off in 1960 with the BBC's *Pinky and Perky Pop Parade* – the duo being as famous for their singing as their distinctive voices. They were also famous for hijacking the BBC with their pirate station, PPC TV (Pinky and Perky Co. Television). Pinky and Perky defected to ITV in 1969 and remained there until 1972, when the Dalibars retired.

When the puppets were on our screens, children could choose from a huge range of toy merchandise including: a Pinky and Perky Animated Snowstorm by manufacturer Linda produced in 1964; a range of puppets from Pelham including a particularly nice one of co-star Morton Frog; Chad Valley children's projectors and slides; a Pinky and Perky Stencil Set by Pinky and Perky Enterprises (1964) Ltd; and of course a variety of money boxes, 'Bendy' toys, books and annuals. As the old joke goes, 'they were stinking rich and living like pigs…'.

Television's Famous Musical Characters

LEFT: Pinky and Perky's real career took off in 1960 with the BBC's *Pinky and Perky Pop Parade*.

ABOVE: 'Pinky and Perky' glove puppets manufactured by Chad Valley.

BELOW: The *Shari Lewis Show* began on US TV in 1960. Lamb Chop was Shari's most famous creation. Tragically, Shari died aged only sixty-five in 1998.

Sooty – Into the Sixties and Beyond

By the 1960s, Sooty's popularity had increased to the extent that creator Harry Corbett had supplemented the mute bear with a range of supporting characters such as Sweep, Sue and Butch. Naturally, Sooty glove puppets were the most popular toy and Chad Valley's were of particularly high quality; collectors should check that Sweep glove puppets still squeak. Interestingly, in March 1962 the BBC broadcast an episode of *Sooty* featuring Pelham puppets of rivals Pinky and Perky. In 1976, Matthew Corbett took over from his father Harry, who died in 1989. Although Matthew has now signed over the rights to Sooty and has also retired, the bear endures, becoming a cartoon character as recently as 1996.

It is beyond the scope of this book to study every successful TV show from the 1960s, so what follows is a small selection of American programmes that enjoyed commercial success with related toy merchandising.

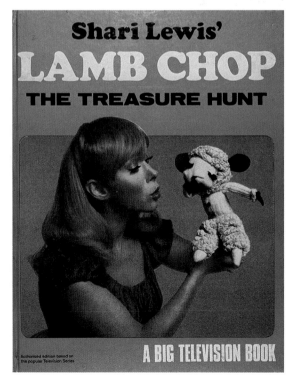

American Adventures

Inspired by the 1961 movie of the same name, *Voyage to the Bottom of the Sea* became one of the most successful TV shows of the 1960s. The story of a nuclear submarine, *Seaview*, and the adventures of its crew, led by Admiral Nelson (played by Walter Pidgeon in the original Irwin Allen film and by Richard Basehart in the TV series) and Captain Crane, *Voyage to the Bottom of the Sea* was first screened on America's ABC Television in 1964 and continued for 110 episodes until 1968. Today, although it is still possible to pick up 'modern' plastic kits, mostly of Japanese origin, of *Seaview* and its smaller Flying Sub, the most collectable are those originally produced by US kit manufacturer Aurora in 1966 and 1968 respectively.

In 1962 a Gold Key comic book entitled *Space Family Robinson* first appeared in the USA. Creators Del Connell and Dan Spiegel had transplanted the famous *Swiss Family Robinson* story into outer space. Later editions of the comic, which had become a regular favourite, included readers' letters suggesting the story be made into a film. In 1965, CBS Television and the above mentioned Irwin Allen obliged with *Lost in Space*, a TV series that was uncannily similar to the Gold Key comics.

VOYAGE TO THE BOTTOM OF THE SEA ANNUAL

AUTHORISED EDITION
Starring RICHARD BASEHART as Admiral Nelson and DAVID HEDISON as Commander Crane

ABOVE: **Starring Richard Basehart as Admiral Nelson and David Hedison as Commander Crane, *Voyage to the Bottom of the Sea* was first broadcast from 1964–68.**

Hollywood star Lloyd Bridges was the star of *Sea Hunt*, broadcast in the USA between 1959 and 1961.

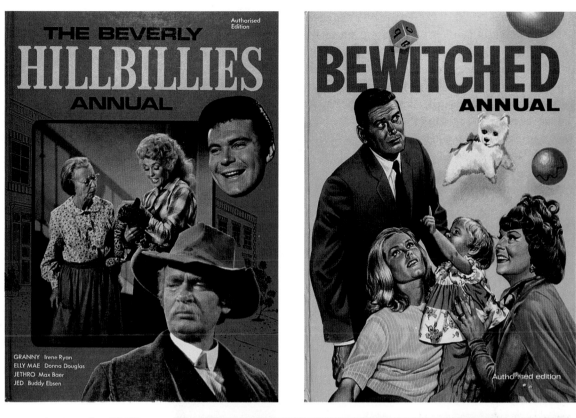

GRANNY Irene Ryan
ELLY MAE Donna Douglas
JETHRO Max Baer
JED Buddy Ebsen

ABOVE: *The Beverly Hillbillies*, a tale of ordinary folk who strike oil, was on our screens from 1962 until 1971.

ABOVE RIGHT: *Bewitched* was on television between 1964 and 1972. The annual shown is an early one from the 1960s.

Aurora Spindrift spaceship from the US TV blockbuster, *Land of the Giants*. This kit was originally produced in 1968.

Lost in Space featured lots of great characters but one of them stands above all others – the famous YM-3 Robot. US kit company Aurora was one of the many manufacturers to obtain a concession allowing production of likenesses of the tracked machine. Its kit, 'The Robot – Lost in Space', first appeared in 1968. The same year, Aurora also produced a great replica of *The Spindrift* spaceship from another blockbuster US TV series, *Land of the Giants*. However, it looked uncannily like the Flying Sub housed in the nose of the *Seaview*, although perhaps this isn't too surprising as, like *Voyage to the Bottom of the Sea*, it was another Irwin Allen production!

Another comic-based TV spin-off was ABC's hit series *Batman*, starring Adam West and Burt Ward as the crime-fighting duo, Batman and Robin. A massive hit when it was first broadcast in January 1966, the original series consisted of 120 episodes and ran until March 1968. Countless *Batman* toys, comics, graphic novels, games, household accessories, trading cards, GAF Viewmaster discs and action figures were produced at the time and there is still a thriving market for all things to do with the Caped Crusader today.

One enduring and highly prized toy is British die-cast manufacturer Corgi's replica of the amazing Batmobile, first produced in 1966. Boxed versions of this classic die-cast are worth many hundreds of pounds, the most valuable being those with red tyres (most were black). The vehicle, based on the Lincoln Futura, a concept car which appeared at the Detroit Motor Show back in 1955, was also available as a die-cast by Husky, one of Corgi's rivals. Plastic model kit manufacturers also produced replicas of the Batmobile. Aurora's 1/32 scale version was released to coincide with the launch of the TV series in 1966. It was one of the company's all-time bestsellers, attracting more than one million pre-sale orders before it was even released.

The following year, Aurora released a 1/12 scale model depicting Batman's nemesis, the Penguin, brandishing his umbrella. Aurora's designers took great care to capture the features of actor Burgess Meredith, who portrayed the Penguin in the TV series. Consequently, it's an excellent and, naturally, very rare model. In 1968, Aurora complemented its enormously successful Batman range with kits of the Batcycle and the Batboat.

Another internationally popular American 1960s TV series that generated a wide range of toy merchandising was *The Monkees*. This series followed the activities of a whacky fun-loving group cast in the mould of the Beatles; indeed, the concept was based on the success of the Fab Four's hit movie, *A Hard Day's Night*.

The Monkees, starring Americans Micky Dolenz (the child star of 1950s TV series *Circus Boy*), Peter Tork and Mike Nesmith as well as Britisher Davy Jones, first aired in September 1966 and continued its run for two years. Being a manufactured band, although the Monkees toured they couldn't escape the rather disparaging nickname of 'the Pre-Fab Four'.

Land of the Giants Television Picture Story Book. **The TV series was first broadcast between 1968 and 1970.**

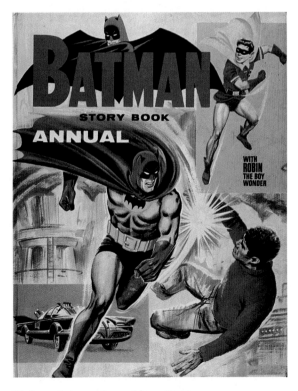

Vintage *Batman Annual* from 1969.

LEFT: *Daktari* began in 1966 and followed the adventures of an American animal doctor, various humans, a cross-eyed lion called Clarence and Judy the chimp on an African game reserve. This annual dates from 1968.

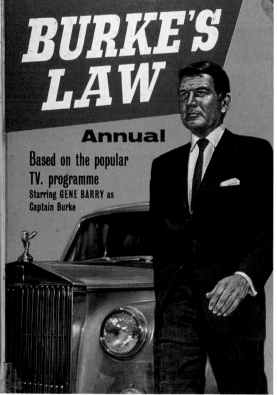

ABOVE: Featuring the crazy antics of four wacky animals, *The Banana Splits* was Hanna-Barbera's first foray into live-action TV (previously the company was famous for its cartoons such as *The Flintstones* and *Top Cat*). *The Banana Splits* was broadcast between 1968 and 1970.

Burke's Law starred Gene Barry and was broadcast between 1963–66.

ABOVE LEFT: *The Monkees Annual* – 'Here They Come! The Swingiest, Zaniest Group on the Scene' – 1967.

ABOVE: Number twenty-seven of *Monkees Monthly*, published in April 1969.

LEFT: Rare Monkeemobile manufactured in the 1960s by Huskey. Kit manufacturer Airfix also produced a replica of the customized GTO Pontiac created by designer Dean Jeffries.

The show was great fun, however, and a wide variety of toy merchandise was produced. The 'fifth star' of the show is arguably the Monkeemobile – the customized GTO Pontiac created by designer Dean Jeffries. Corgi, Husky and even Airfix produced scale replicas of the classic vehicle.

James Bond

One of the biggest movie phenomena of all time began in the 1960s – that of licensed-to-kill secret agent 007, James Bond. And with the enduring success of the films, the range of licensed merchandise has continued to grow as well.

Beginning with *Dr. No* in 1962, followed in 1963 by *From Russia With Love,* by *Goldfinger* in 1964 and *Thunderball* in 1965, by the mid-1960s Sean Connery's character had triggered a flood of Bond-related merchandising, which continues to this day. The 007 films also generated huge interest in spy- and espionage-related programmes, leading indirectly to programmes such as *The Man From U.N.C.L.E.* and, later in the decade, *Danger Man*, *The Champions*, *The Prisoner* and *The Persuaders*.

British plastic-kit giant Airfix was very quick to agree licence arrangements with 007 rights owners, Eon and Glidrose. In 1965, the manufacturer released its first 007 kit, a 1/12 scale diorama depicting James Bond and the bowler-hatted (but what a bowler hat) Odd Job. Because of the licence restrictions on all movie-related products, this kit was only around for a few years and surviving examples (boxed and unbuilt, of course) attract enormous prices on the collectors' market. Airfix re-released the kit in the late 1990s, but it was clearly inferior as regards packaging compared to the original model and didn't do too much to dent prices. Its reappearance did, at least, enable keen modellers to recreate the classic encounter of the *Goldfinger* adversaries without resorting to the sacrilege of actually constructing a rare original.

The next two 007-related kits from Airfix were first available in 1967, when the company produced a stunning 1/24 scale replica of Bond's gadget-laden Aston Martin DB5 and a tiny replica of the secret agent's

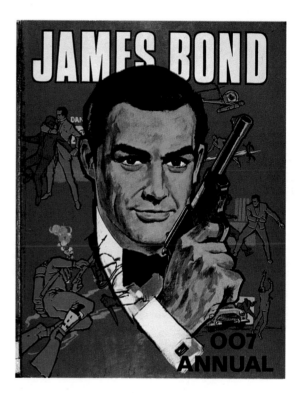

ABOVE: Collectable *James Bond 007 Annual* from 1966.

LEFT: **Original and very rare Airfix kit of James Bond and Odd Job from 1965. This 1/12 scale kit was re-released in the 1990s. The assembled figures stand alongside.**

Trio of very collectable 007 figures made in the 1960s by US manufacturer Gilbert.

ABOVE: 'Little Nellie' in all her glory!

RIGHT: From 1967, Airfix's replica of 007's rocket-firing Wallis Autogyro, 'Little Nellie'.

rocket-firing Wallis autogyro, 'Little Nellie'. This later replica of one of the 'co-stars' of the hit film *You Only Live Twice* was also re-released by Airfix in the 1990s. Despite this, however, original kits still command upwards of £350.

The final Airfix Bond kit was released in 1968. It was a detailed 1/24 scale replica of the Toyota 2000 GT, again from *You Only Live Twice*, which was made at Pinewood in London and partly on location in Japan.

Airfix wasn't the only plastic construction kit manufacturer to produce high-quality models based on the 007 movies. American manufacturer Aurora released a 1/25 scale Aston Martin DB5 in 1965. However, because Airfix had obtained the licence to manufacture model replicas of the vehicle, Aurora's product was called the 'Aston Martin Super Spy Car'. Although it was identical in every way to the vehicle Bond drove (ejector seat, bullet-proof armoured shield and so on), there was no mention of 007 anywhere on the packaging.

Two years later, with the licence agreement presumably signed, Aurora also produced a great 1/8 scale diorama featuring Sean Connery, gun in hand, firing from behind the cover of a brick wall. The same year, the company also produced an equally good representation of Odd Job, about to launch his lethal bowler hat in the direction of its next victim.

Naturally, the 007 franchises generated a huge number of licensed toys in the 1960s; for example, shoulder-holstered cap-firing guns, attaché cases, toy Berettas, Walthers and Lugers with removable silencers, cars, walkie-talkies, colouring books and countless games and puzzles proliferated.

1/24th. SCALE

AIRFIX

007 JAMES BOND'S AUTOGYRO

Airfix James Bond Toyota 2000 GT from the movie *You Only Live Twice*, released in 1968.

Stunning original 1/24 scale replica of Bond's gadget-laden Aston Martin DB5 manufactured by Airfix in 1967.

American manufacturer Gilbert released 12in (305mm) dolls and a range of smaller figures depicting Bond and his adversaries in a variety of outfits. Surviving examples of any of these toys are extremely expensive, even more so if they are in their original boxes (or, in the case of the smaller figures, still mounted on their card backings) and complete with all accessories. For example, Gilbert's 1965 vintage James Bond doll from the film *Thunderball* should come with an alloy gun in a separate envelope, a mask, snorkel, two pairs of fins, trunks and shorts, plus a set of instructions explaining how the components all fit together. As readers might imagine, mint and boxed examples of the above sell for upwards of £500.

The same year, Gilbert released a range of different 007 toys. They are all rare; however, a personal favourite of mine is the James Bond Spy Watch, which featured 'secret sighting lenses' and a 'world time guide'. Another rarity to look out for is the 007 Code-o-matic secret coding and decoding machines, produced in the mid-1960s by a variety of toy manufacturers.

In 1966, US manufacturer American Character produced an interesting set that featured a 007 Action Pen and Vaper Paper, a material that enabled kids to write and reveal secret messages. Vaper Paper was all the rage in 1960s America and was to be resurrected for toys associated with other 'spy' programmes such as *The Man From U.N.C.L.E.*

Meanwhile, British youngsters could play with the exciting James Bond 007 Secret Service game, manufactured by Spears Games in 1965. However, Britain also produced perhaps the most coveted and collectable James Bond toy of all time – Corgi's Aston Martin DB5. Based on an existing DB4 already in its range, Corgi (Mettoy) released its version of Bond's vehicle in November 1965.

Corgi's design engineers created a special test rig to ensure that working features – most notably an operating ejector seat, extended rear-facing armoured shield and machine guns that popped out from the front bumper – all worked perfectly. Their efforts resulted in the toy winning the vote for 'Toy of the Year 1965' from the British Toy Retailers Association. In its first three years of production, more than 3,000,000 examples of this toy vehicle were sold. On the original packaging the vehicle was depicted in silver finish. Due to its premium status (certainly Corgi's manufacturing skills had been tested to the maximum), it was, however, released in a gold finish.

Three years later, Corgi did indeed produce a silver version of the DB5. However, it was slightly larger than its predecessor and included even more features, such as rotating number plates and evil-looking hub-mounted tyre slashers. Although released late, it is worth considerably more than the gold-coloured version. Not surprisingly, being a perennial favourite a variety of models based on Corgi's DB5 original tools and the designs of other manufacturers of the vehicle can still be purchased, but surviving examples of the original toys, even without their boxes, are worth far more than any recent replicas.

Small-Screen Secret Agents

The success of James Bond led to the migration of secret agents into our living rooms via the television. One of the most successful of these programmes was America's *The Man From U.N.C.L.E.*, with Napoleon Solo and Illya Kuryakin (respectively actors Robert Vaughn and David McCallum) bursting onto the scene in 1964 as agents of the United Network Command for Law Enforcement. Working for boss Mr Waverley, the duo combated the evil activities of THRUSH (the Technological Hierarchy for the Removal of Undesirables and the Subjugation of Humanity – thank goodness for acronyms). The series was broadcast until 1968 and was such a hit that toys, annuals and model kits were quickly licensed.

One of the most collectable toys based on the series is Corgi's Thrushbuster. This Oldsmobile came in blue or white and, with a push of a roof-mounted button, Solo and Kuryakin would take turns in popping out of the side windows to take pot shots at their enemies. Boxed examples of this vehicle are extremely rare and if they still include the prized 'Waverley ring' can expect to sell for £200–£300 at the time of writing.

Manufacturers including Marx, Ideal and AC Gilbert signed merchandising agreements to produce *Man From U.N.C.L.E.* pistols and shoulder holsters, attaché cases, figures from the series and even a cigarette lighter that doubled as a radio and pistol. Milton Bradley (MB) and other games manufacturers produced a range of spy-related board games.

In 1966, US kit giant Aurora produced a couple of lovely 1/12 scale cameos of agents Solo and Kuryakin set in suitably dramatic dioramas. These are very rare in America and 'scarcer than hen's teeth' on this side of the Atlantic.

Rare *The Man From U.N.C.L.E.* annual from 1966.

A BRIEF HISTORY OF CORGI

The Corgi brand can trace its lineage back to the 1936 when Mettoy (metal toys) was founded. Mettoy launched the Corgi brand of die-cast toy vehicles in 1956. The enormous success of Corgi encouraged Mettoy to go public in 1963. Despite its initial success, however, Mettoy went into receivership in 1983. Fortunately, an MBO management buy-out rescued the Corgi brand name.

One of the most collectable toys based on *The Man From U.N.C.L.E.* series is Corgi's 1966 Thrushbuster.

BELOW: The rarest and most collectable *The Man From U.N.C.L.E.* associated annuals actually belong to the *The Girl From U.N.C.L.E.* – an offshoot of the main series, which starred actress Stephanie Powers as April Dancer.

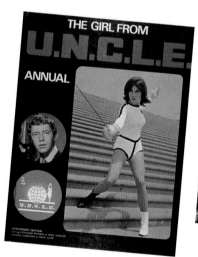

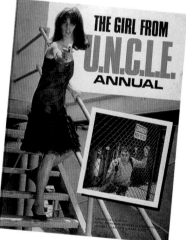

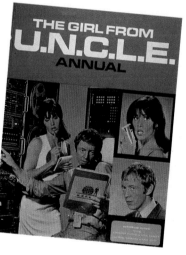

Naturally, *The Man From U.N.C.L.E.* books and annuals proliferated. The rarest are those produced in association with *The Girl From U.N.C.L.E.*, an offshoot of the main series, which starred actress Stephanie Powers as April Dancer.

The Avengers, another classic TV series in a similar (but different) vein to James Bond, began life in 1961. Originally, its star was British actor Ian Hendry, play-ing Dr David Keel, who enlisted the services of John Steed (Patrick McNee) to help him solve a murder. By the second season, however, it was clear that McNee's mysterious character – did he, or didn't he work for the British secret service? – was the draw of the show. When anthropologist and judo exponent Dr Cathy Gale (Honor Blackman) partnered him, a clear and successful formula had been established.

The Avengers annual dating from 1969.

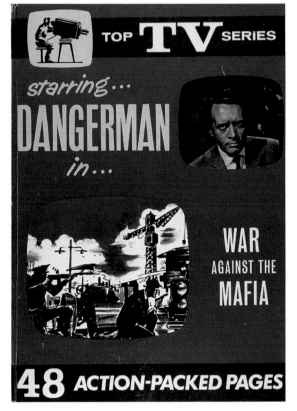

Dangerman, starring Patrick McGoohan
as John Drake, ran from 1964 until 1966.

The original *Avengers* series ran until 1969 and during that time Steed was also famously partnered by Emma Peel (Diana Rigg) and Tara King (Linda Thorson).

A wide range of *Avengers* toys and game tie-ins were produced and in 1964 Blackman and McNee even released a song, 'Kinky Boots', referring to the nickname given to the long leather boots Blackman often wore in the series. In 1966 Corgi produced a stunning gift set comprising John Steed's red Bentley (What else would one have expected the bowler-hatted, umbrella-carrying toff to drive?) and Emma Peel's white Lotus Elan.

Equally whacky, but in a very different and quintessentially British way, was Patrick McGoohan's *The Prisoner*, his follow up to *Dangerman*. *The Prisoner* was set in a surreal prison in which inmate No 6 (McGoohan), a secret agent, is held against his will for having attempted to resign from the service. The series, broadcast in 1967 and 1968, included some outlandish and unsettling ingredients. There were spherical prison guardians called Rovers, capable of appearing at random and, if they so wished, of smothering any escapee. Although McGoohan's car is seen to be a very trendy Lotus Seven Series II sports car in the opening titles, after he arrives at his prison (really the picturesque Welsh holiday destination of Portmeirion), the most common vehicle seen is the equally new and trendy Mini Moke. The creator of the Mini car, Sir Alec Issigonis, designed this vehicle, whose name means 'Donkey', in 1959.

In 1968 Dinky Toys produced a stunning replica of the Mini Moke, complete with red and white striped canopy and the famous penny-farthing emblem on the engine bonnet. Mint and boxed versions of this die-cast toy are very rare and being of a relatively delicate construction the canopy and its supports are often broken on those examples that have survived without the protection of the original box.

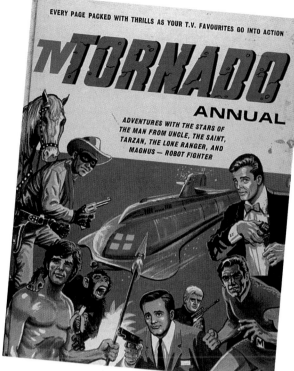

ABOVE: *TV Tornado Annual*
from the late 1960s featuring *The Man
From U.N.C.L.E.*, *The Saint*, *Bonanza*, *The Green
Hornet*, *Tarzan*, *The Phantom*, *Flash Gordon*, *Magnus
Robot Fighter* and *Voyage to the Bottom of the Sea.*

Mission: Impossible
annual from 1967. The original TV series
was first broadcast between 1966 and 1973.

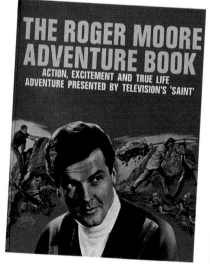

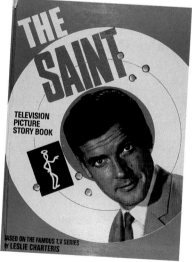

The Roger Moore Adventure Book.
'Action, Excitement and True Life
Adventure Presented by Television's
"Saint"', dating from 1966.

*The Saint Television
Picture Story Book*
from 1969.

Men on the Moon

Aside from the 1962 Cuban Missile Crisis, the assassination the following year of American President John F. Kennedy and the US civil rights protests, which not surprisingly have very little relevance to a book about film- and TV-related toy collectables – although in 1965 Aurora did release a very collectable 1/8 scale character study of a seated President Kennedy in its 'Great American Presidents' series – arguably the two most memorable media events of the 1960s, each showing mankind's strengths and failings, were the 1969 Apollo Moon landings and the Vietnam War.

The Apollo programme and its predecessor the Gemini programme were largely the result of Kennedy's determination that America should regain the lead in the space race following the upsets caused in the previous decade by the Soviets' apparent lead after their successes with *Sputnik*.

Naturally, the developments of the National Aeronautics and Space Administration (NASA) encouraged a boom in space toys. Some were fanciful and merely rehashes in different packaging of those fantasy items produced during the height of the Cold War paranoia of the 1950s – ray guns, flying saucers, unrealistic rockets and the like.

Plastic construction kit manufacturers produced the most realistic representations of the new developments, although manufacturers such as Lindberg and Aurora couldn't help producing a range of UFOs and flying saucers from the more far-fetched imaginations of their kit designers (although a model of a UFO from the TV series *The Invaders* is a classic).

It is beyond the scope of this book to go into too much detail about the more accurate space models produced in the 1960s and I would point readers in the direction of Mat Irvine's great book, *Creating Space*, should they wish to know more. However, below I've attempted to highlight some of the best.

Following on from its range of kits depicting examples from America's missile arsenal and replicas of the experimental X-Planes that broke the sound barrier and then helped US scientists prepare for operations beyond the stratosphere, American kit company Revell, then based in California, produced replicas of craft from the country's developing space programme.

Beginning with a 1/105 scale replica of a Mercury/Redstone rocket, launch equipment and ground crew in 1962, by 1964 Revell had in its catalogue a 1/48 scale replica of a Mercury/Gemini capsule with an astronaut inside. By 1965 Revell's programme numbered an even larger, 1/24 scale Gemini capsule including two figures and complete with a set of the NASA decals. In 1967 Revell released its first kit of the combined Apollo orbiter and lunar lander. It was produced in 1/96 scale and is eminently collectable.

According to Revell historian, the American author Thomas Graham, for the Christmas season of 1969 to commemorate the lunar landings, Revell marketing director Dave Fisher proposed that the firm produce a large replica of the entire Saturn V assembly. Revell's truly gigantic Apollo Saturn V Moon Rocket was moulded in 1/96 scale and featured a tiny replica of the lunar lander within the nose section. Actually, rival US kit manufacturer Monogram (today happily in partnership with Revell) had produced a 1/144 scale Saturn V assembly in 1968, but it was nowhere near as faithful to the real design as Revell's 1/96 scale offering.

British manufacturer Airfix also managed to get a very good kit of the Saturn V into the shops in time for the Moon landings. Like Monogram's offering, this was much smaller than the Revell kit and was moulded in 1/144 scale. Unlike the Monogram offering, however, it was very accurate indeed. John Gray, Airfix's managing director at the time, insisted that his designers have access to the best drawings available and whatever unclassified photographs they could get hold of.

All the major manufacturers of kits in the 1960s produced individual replicas of the various components of the Apollo programme, including the Lunar Excursion Module (LEM) and orbiter, as well as rather impressionable representations of as yet untried technology such as the jet packs and lunar exploration equipment. Many manufacturers included dioramas of the actual Apollo 11 landing on 20 July 1969. Airfix's 1/72 scale Apollo Lunar Module kit featured a section of the Moon's surface and a tiny representation of the 'Stars and Bars' as placed there by Neil Armstrong and 'Buzz' Aldrin. Airfix's kit could be readily supplemented by figures and accessories, including a Lunar Rover vehicle, in the fifty-seven-piece set of polythene HO-OO Astronauts.

Because, as every Airfix fan knows, these cheap and accessible figures are relatively soft and pliable, when they were first released *Airfix Magazine* recommended that purchasers coated the figures with PVA glue prior to painting and attempting to incorporate them with the 1/72 scale Lunar Module. Sticking them to the polystyrene base was altogether another matter!

Toy Offshoots from the Vietnam War

The other major event that consumed the media's attention throughout the 1960s and beyond, the Vietnam War, is a much less creditable demonstration of man's determination to harness technology to achieve a chosen aim – the American effort to thwart the spread of Communism in South-east Asia. Although American combat troops were deployed in Vietnam, albeit somewhat covertly, as early as 1959, it wasn't until the mid-1960s that the United States became embroiled in an increasingly intractable full-scale war.

It's debatable that the war ever really received the full support of the American people and it certainly didn't have it during the late 1960s. Indeed, most observers agree that any chance of victory was made untenable by the combination of the new personal freedoms enjoyed by US and other citizens during this period – especially at the height of the progressive 'Flower Power' movement at the end of the decade – with the unrivalled freedom of the media to report and record the war for virtually instantaneous television broadcast.

But toy companies are fortunately largely divorced from politics and although these days it's unlikely that toy manufacturers would be willing or able to create as many 'war toys' as companies did in the 1960s, those that were produced then were seen as part of America's patriotic war effort.

Probably the most patriotic expression in toy form was the introduction of the GI Joe action figure in North America. Manufactured by Hasbro, GI Joe, or, to use the correct US Army nomenclature, General Issue Joe, first appeared in North American shops in 1964. It was a huge success and proved that boys would play with… dolls (sorry, action figures!).

Action Man, the British incarnation of the famous 12in (305mm) fighting man, was manufactured in Britain by Hasbro subsidiary Palitoy and was in the shops by 1966. Allegedly, a new name was chosen because 'GI' was considered to be meaningless in the UK. *Dangerman*, starring Patrick McGoohan, was all the rage on British TV at the time; Action Man was created in the vein of McGoohan's character. Action Man was voted 'Toy of the Year 1966' by the British Toy Retailers Association.

Manufacturers of plastic kits had a field day producing replicas of the vehicles and aircraft people saw in almost daily war action on their TVs. American manufacturers such as Monogram, Revell, Lindberg and Aurora naturally led the way.

The Vietnam War was the first real demonstration of the helicopter's all-round military capability. During the Korean War, helicopters had been used largely as logistic workhorses and for transporting wounded soldiers to field hospitals.

For many people, the Bell Huey helicopter is the iconic design of the Vietnam War. Many manufacturers featured them in their ranges, but Revell's 1/24 scale Bell Huey Attack Helicopters were some of the best produced at the time. Revell's first box for one of these kits featured a couple of such machines firing rockets against a painting of a serene sunset and a sailing junk, smoke billowing from its hull. 'The First Air Cavalry Rides Shotgun in the Bell Huey Attack Helicopter' screamed the copy above the illustration. The First Cavalry's distinctive yellow and black shield with inset horse's head was also there for good measure.

A BRIEF HISTORY OF HASBRO

Hasbro was founded by the Hassenfeld brothers in 1923 and has gone on to become one of the largest toy corporations in the world, currently owning MB Games and the latter's famous subsidiary Playskool Inc. In 1991, Hasbro also purchased the famous Tonka and Kenner/Parker brands.

Revell also produced creditable replicas of another helicopter, the giant Sikorsky 'Jolly Green Giant', as well as kits of another classic from the period, the LTV A-7D Corsair II. All were portrayed in battle over the deltas and paddy fields of Indo-China.

US firm Hawk featured an elaborate model in 1/48 scale ('quarter scale' to American modellers), of the distinctive reconnaissance aircraft, the OV-10A Bronco. Again, photos on the box lid showed it in operation above the paddy terraces.

In 1971 Airfix released a good replica of an American carrier-borne F-4B Phantom II in 1/72 scale. It was depicted being launched from one of the US Navy's carriers stationed off the coast of Vietnam.

By this time, the tide of American public opinion was turning dramatically against the war, fuelled by the enormous number of US service casualties. When appearing at civic functions, Revell's founder Lew Glaser would regularly be asked why the company made so many 'war toys'. The stock answer was always 'If you don't buy them, we won't make them', recalled his wife Royle years later. The truth was, civilian subjects just didn't sell, despite the war's growing unpopularity.

However, even Aurora, a company that for years had packed its ranges with patriotic figures of soldiers, sailors and airmen, had to concede that the writing was on the wall for overtly militaristic subjects. Aurora's 1/12 scale depiction of an Armalite-wielding Green Beret lasted barely a year before it was withdrawn. The company's far less controversial 1/15 scale diorama, 'Flag Raising at Iwo Jima', released the same year, was more acceptable but no less patriotic. One might have thought the producers of John Wayne's 1968 Vietnam epic, *The Green Berets* – 'They had to be the toughest fighting force on Earth – and the men who led them had to be just a little bit tougher!' – would have been equally good at gauging the general public's mood. They weren't.

Film Spin-Offs

The top ten cinema box office hits during the 1960s saw Walt Disney's *One Hundred and One Dalmatians* released in 1961 as the biggest grossing movie of the decade. *Dr. No* and *From Russia With Love*, the first two Bond movies, didn't make it into the top ten but *Goldfinger*, *Thunderball* and *You Only Lived Twice* did. Children's classic *The Jungle Book* (1967) was the second ranking movie, while *The Sound of Music* (1965) stood at third place. *Mary*

This Dinky Toys Ju 87 Stuka dive-bomber was manufactured in 1969 and was one of the many items licensed from Guy Hamilton's *Battle of Britain* movie. It was underslung with a cap-firing bomb!

British kit manufacturer FROG produced a series of licensed plastic construction kits featuring existing items from their range, boxed and branded with Spitfire Production's striking movie branding.

BELOW: The Arab–Israeli Six-Day War took place in June 1967. The massively successful Israeli air attacks attracted world attention. Airfix produced a 1/72 scale kit of an Israeli Mirage and an Egyptian MiG-15 in its famous 1960s 'Dog Fight Doubles' range.

LEFT: The lovely Ann-Margret graces the cover of this March 1967 edition of the popular film magazine, *Photoplay*. The ephemera of the 'TV generation' – the magazines and periodicals that document the various landmark films and TV programmes that have entertained audiences for decades – are becoming more and more collectable.

BELOW: 'The Jungle Book Game', available at the time of the film's first release in 1967.

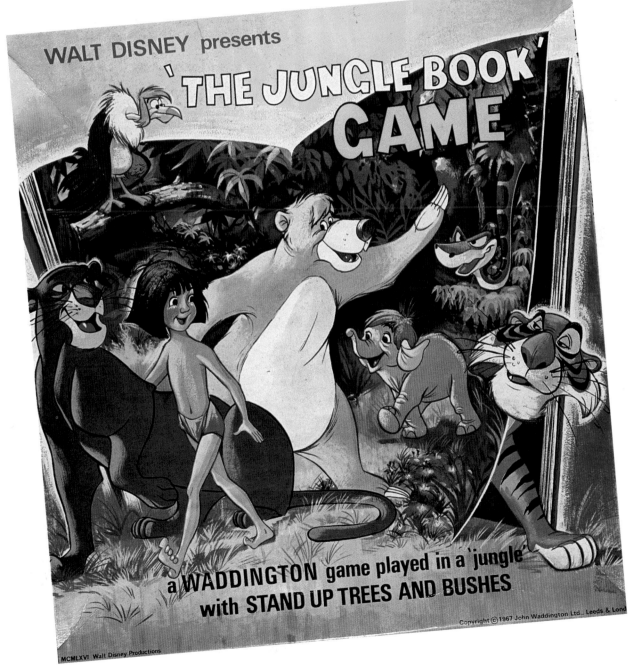

ABOVE: *Mary Poppins Souvenir Song Album* from 1964.

ABOVE: Rare in its original packaging, this Airfix plastic construction kit of the Pan-Am 'Orion' Spacecraft as featured in Stanley Kubrick's classic 1968 movie, *2001: A Space Odyssey*, was released by the famous British manufacturer in 1969. Though re-released several time in the 1970s and 1980s, early examples like this are much sought after by the growing ranks of collectors of film and TV-related kits.

BELOW: Surviving Viewmaster reels are very collectable. This one, by Sawyers, features twenty-one views from Julie Andrews' hit film *Mary Poppins*, which came to cinema screens in 1964.

The original *Planet of the Apes* movie was released in 1968. This 'Super Scenes' diorama in a bottle kit was produced in association with the movie by US manufacturer Addar.

BELOW: This *Planet of the Apes* jigsaw puzzle was one of the many licensed products available when the film was on general release in the late 1960s.

ABOVE: **Dick Van Dyke, in-between roles (*Mary Poppins* in 1964 and *Chitty Chitty Bang Bang* in 1968).**

Poppins (1964) was at number ten. Surprisingly, movies such as *Chitty Chitty Bang Bang*, released in 1968, Rex Harrison's *Doctor Dolittle* (1967), Stanley Kubrick's *2001: A Space Odyssey* (1968) and *Battle of Britain* (1969) – all movies with very successful toy or model tie-ins – didn't make the top ten.

American kit manufacturer Aurora released a 1/25 scale construction kit of Chitty in 1968. Today it is coveted by kit collectors. The original 1968 Corgi die-cast of Caractacus Potts' fantastic vehicle is another 'must have', but a very expensive collectable. Fortunately, in 1998, the manufacturer re-released the vehicle, using the original mould tools and including the original working feature of movable wings. The

ABOVE: *Chitty Chitty Bang Bang* jigsaw puzzle from 1968. Keen-eyed readers will notice the names 'Eon' and 'Albert Broccoli' – the owners of the Bond franchise; *Chitty Chitty Bang Bang* was written by 007 creator Ian Fleming.

LEFT: *Chitty Chitty Bang Bang* souvenir brochure from 1968.

This bendable 'Doctor Dolittle and Polynesia the Parrot' was made by US manufacturer Mattel. Produced in association with the 1967 movie, it is now extremely rare and very collectable.

ABOVE: This *Doctor Dolittle Press-Out Book* cost only 2/6 (12.5p) when it was first available in 1967. It's worth considerably more now.

The *Battle of Britain* epic released in 1969 spawned lots of merchandised tie-ins like this puzzle.

release was scheduled to coincide with the staging of the new stage musical at the London Palladium.

In 1967 Mattel released a 'bendable and poseable' figure of 'Doctor Dolittle and Polynesia the Parrot'. The likeness to Rex Harrison captured in such a small figure was astounding.

The *Battle of Britain* epic was naturally a huge stimulus to kit manufacturers and models of Spitfires, Heinkels and Messerschmitts flew off the shelves. British manufacturer FROG had obtained the licence from United Artists to package some of its existing replicas in special boxes emblazoned with the film's distinctive branding. Britain's Dinky Toys released a range of die-cast Spitfires and Messerschmitts featuring the film's branding. Boxed examples can still be found. Be sure to check that the Stuka, the third replica in the Dinky range, retains its cap-firing bomb.

Amongst the many products sold under licence to the producers of Stanley Kubrick's *2001* was a neat Airfix kit of the 216in (5,490mm) long Pan Am Orion Space Clipper Shuttle as seen in the film. Ironically, Pan Am proper never actually made it into the twenty-first century, the original airline collapsing in 1991.

Aurora produced some 1/144 scale versions of the Pan Am Clipper too. However, another Aurora release is one of the most rare *2001* kits. In 1968 the company manufactured a 1/55 kit of the Moon Bus – 'From the Movie of the Century' claimed the box graphics.

War films released during the 1960s naturally had a large effect upon the sale of toy soldiers and die-cast military vehicles and aircraft. They were also a great stimulus to kit manufacturers. Although there was a shift towards more cynical portrayals of martial derring-do, especially in films like *The Dirty Dozen* (1967) and *The Bridge at Remagen* (1969), other films depicted the traditional stories of heroism and toughness. Remaining blockbuster movies in this sector include *The Guns of Navarone* (1961), *The Longest Day* (1962), *633 Squadron* (1964) and *Where Eagles Dare* (1968).

There was a resurgence of interest in military modelling during the 1960s – not just in tanks and other armoured fighting vehicles (AFVs), but in the field of model soldiers, especially those in 54mm scale (1/32). This was partly due to the influence of films such as *Zulu* (1964) and *The Charge of the Light Brigade* (1968), but also because of the hype surrounding the imminent release of Sergei Bondarchuk's epic, *Waterloo*, in 1970.

ABOVE: **Marvellously evocative Dinky Toys Spitfire MkII from the 1969 epic,** *Battle of Britain*. **A tiny electric motor concealed in the aircraft's nose enabled the propeller to spin!**

RIGHT: **The film** *Those Magnificent Men in Their Flying Machines* **premiered in 1965. Short-lived British manufacturer Inpact was quick to capitalize on the success of the film. However, careful study shows that the company didn't use the actual movie branding – perhaps it never applied for the concession!**

THE 1970s: TOP TV, THE BIG MOVIES, MEDIA EVENTS

War Was Big Business

Although it hadn't secured the licence, and therefore the models could not be linked directly to the film, in an attempt to capitalize on the commercial success of the 1970 movie *Waterloo*, British kit manufacturer Airfix released a range of HO-OO products based on the famous 1815 battle. These soldiers, mostly moulded in cream polythene, were what every boy needed if he was going to recreate Napoleon's storming of Le Haye Saint farm, defended by Wellington's allied troops. Airfix

Souvenir programme to Sergei Bondarchuk's 1970 epic, *Waterloo*.

manufactured HO-OO artillery, cavalry and a reasonable replica of the famous Belgian farmhouse too.

With Rod Steiger and Christopher Plummer's *Waterloo*, the 1970s began with an epic of blockbuster proportions. For children growing up at this time – especially boys – the succession of big war films – *Where Eagles Dare*, *Battle of Britain* and now *Waterloo* – were deemed to have been made simply so that we could get maximum play value from toys. Action Man, plastic soldiers, quality toy guns like Mattel's M-16 Marauder and the daddy of them all, Topper Toys' Johnny Seven, were the essential props in our highly personal recreations of such epics.

Topper's Johnny Seven first appeared in 1964, but was a much-loved toy for years afterwards. It is a highly desirable collectable today and even unboxed versions with missing accessories command huge prices on auction sites like eBay. Johnny Seven OMA (One Man Army) was its full name. The large and cumbersome toy ('multi-function machine gun'!) was moulded in green plastic and came complete with an arsenal of weapons. There were grenades, 'anti-bunker' missiles, armour-piercing rounds and, if you were cornered by a bunch of kids with Mattel Marauders, a detachable pistol so that you could take one of the enemy with you and then commit suicide. No one with a Johnny Seven was ever taken alive.

Blue Peter Versus *Magpie*

War toys' aside, children's attention was also directed to some more wholesome entertainments. Though it is hard to believe, BBC's *Blue Peter*, a children's TV staple that took its name from the flag worn on a ship

Captain Pugwash Annual from 1976.

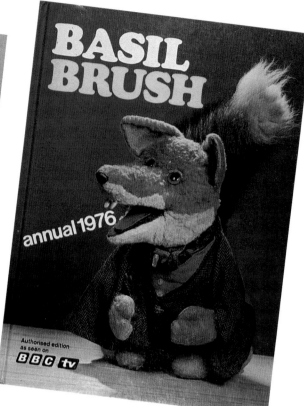

ABOVE: *Basil Brush Annual 1976*: 'Boom, Boom!'

The weekly *Look-in* magazine was billed as the 'Junior *TV Times*'. The cover of this edition from 1974 features *Man About the House* stars Richard O'Sullivan (Robin Tripp), Paula Wilcox (Chrissy) and Sally Thomsett, who played Jo.

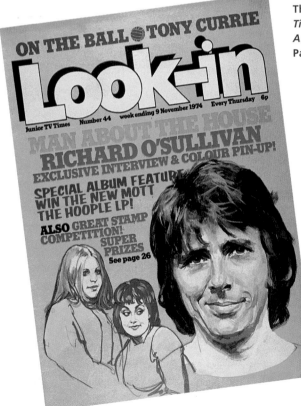

beginning a voyage, was launched in 1958. From then until the late 1960s, it ruled the (TV air) waves. Producer Biddy Baxter changed presenters regularly, from the earliest days of Christopher Trace and Leila Williams to arguably the most famous trio of all, Valerie Singleton, John Noakes and Peter Purves, who guided the show from the mid-1960s well into the 1970s.

Blue Peter was good patrician fare, the producers ensuring that the highest standards were upheld. Or at least they did until London Zoo elephant Lulu relieved itself live in the studio during a 1969 edition. Children intently followed the presenters' demonstrations of how to make a desk-tidy or a jumbo jet from empty detergent bottles and sticky-backed plastic. 'Here's one we made earlier,' uttered John Noakes, as Petra the Alsatian, intent on maximizing her TV exposure, ran off with the PVA glue.

RIGHT: This *Tiswas Annual* dates from 1979. The show was on air between 1974–82.

FAR RIGHT: Presented by Chris Tarrant and the comely Sally James during the show's heyday, *Tiswas* brought mayhem to children's TV. Kids loved it and even adults were eventually won round. *Tiswas* also helped to launch comedian Lenny Henry's career and who could forget Bob Carolgees and Spit the Dog or the antics of John Gorman. This version of the Tiswas Phantom Flyer was actually produced just as the show was coming to an end in 1981 but it's typical of the sort of licensed merchandise available during the 1970s.

RIGHT: *Magpie Annual 1974*. Rock 'n' roll!

By 1970, however, *Blue Peter*'s hegemony was challenged by a serious rival. *Magpie,* similar but different, was British Independent Television's treatment of the same format (three presenters, pets, adventurous excursions to foreign parts and thing to make and do).

Magpie was first broadcast on ITV channel Thames TV's first day of operation – 30 July 1968. In its first year it was broadcast only once a week but afterwards was on twice weekly like *Blue Peter.*

Compared to *Blue Peter, Magpie* was rock 'n' roll. After all, one of its first presenters, Pete Brady, was a former Radio 1 DJ. He left in 1972 when the show settled down to be presented by Susan Stranks, Douglas Rae and Mick Robertson. Along with other boys on the cusp of puberty, I particularly liked Ms Stranks because she never wore a bra. And Mick Robertson was particularly popular with girls because he looked like Marc Bolan from T.Rex, a 'glam-rock' band at the height of its fame in 1972. When Susan Stranks left the show in 1974 she was replaced by the equally comely Jenny Hanley, daughter of actor and latterly TV presenter Jimmy Hanley.

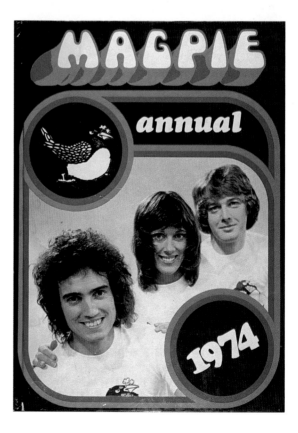

But despite its funkier format, *Magpie* was no match for the Dreadnought flying the Blue Peter and in 1980 it sank without trace. *Blue Peter* is still very much with us and now in its sixth decade!

A tradition with both programmes was the publication of annuals featuring highlights of the previous year's broadcasts. Early editions are now very collectable. The first *Blue Peter Annual* was published in 1964. This edition is especially valuable, but the first dozen or so that followed it also command very respectable prices. *Magpie*'s first annual was published in the show's inaugural year, 1969.

Perhaps the most collectable items from either show is the famous *Blue Peter* badge, available in a range of colours from the 'standard' blue ship on a white plastic shield to the rarest gold-plated version awarded to children who have exhibited acts of bravery and courage.

Early in 2006 *Blue Peter* badges were in the news for all the wrong reasons when it was discovered that they were being traded. The fact that wearers of these badges may not have earned them in the traditional way but still enjoyed free entry to certain visitor attractions drew widespread condemnation.

A *Wombles Annual* from 1974 ...

... and an original Orinoco Womble from the same period belonging to Martell Mitchell, who cherished him as much as her father did his World Cup Willie mascot nearly ten years previously. This toy was manufactured by Burbank Toys of England and is complete with a working voicebox.

Worzel Gummidge starred ex Doctor Who Jon Pertwee and was broadcast between 1979–81.

RIGHT: **This Arrow Games jigsaw puzzle was produced in the 1970s under licence from Serge Danot's famous BBC TV series, *The Magic Roundabout*.**

BELOW LEFT: *Jim'll Fix It Annual* **from 1979 (the popular BBC TV show presented by the legendary Jimmy Savile began in 1975).**

BELOW RIGHT: *Supersonic Annual* **from 1978 featuring silver-haired supreme, Mike Mansfield, who introduced, produced and directed the show and showcased 'live' performances from 1970s pop groups as he sat behind an enormous mixing desk: 'Cue VT!'**

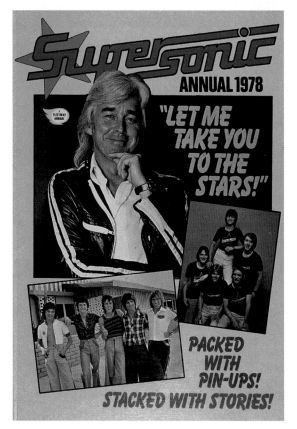

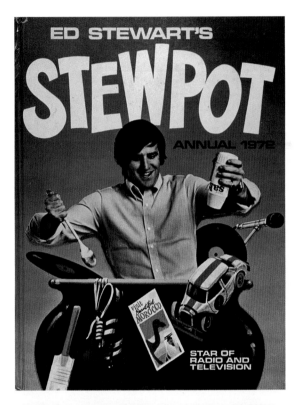

ABOVE LEFT: *Ed Stewart's Stewpot Annual 1972*. Ed Stewart was part of the original Radio One line up when the station launched in 1967. He made his mark in the 1970s presenting BBC Radio Two's children's programme, *Junior Choice*. He's still with BBC Radio after forty years!

ABOVE: This Mr Smash clockwork walking Martian by Marx Toys was inspired by the TV commercial for Cadbury's Smash instant mashed potato. Similarly with items licensed from films or TV programmes, characters featuring in commercials are also very collectable. Mr Smash toys are very collectable. It's quite difficult to find them complete with their original boxes, like the one shown here. However, although the example shown still has its potato in its 'hand', it is missing its antennae – generally the first thing to get lost or damaged.

LEFT: *Catweazle*, an eccentric Saxon hermit played by actor Geoffrey Bayldon, had his own British TV series in 1970–71. This annual dates from 1971.

The presenters of *Blue Peter* and *Magpie* weren't the only wholesome children's entertainers on television in the early 1970s. Clive Dunn, Corporal Jones of BBC TV's *Dad's Army*, topped the charts at Christmas 1970 and into January of the new year with his smash hit, 'Grandad'.

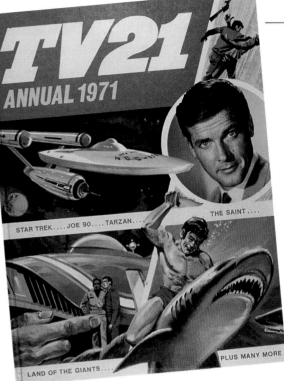

ABOVE: *Gerry Anderson's UFO Annual*; Century 21 Merchandising Ltd, 1970.

BELOW: *Thunderbirds Annual* from 1971. How cool is T2?

ABOVE: Well into the 1970s, *TV21 Annuals* continued to sell in large numbers. This edition is from 1971.

BELOW: Available between 1967 and 1973, Dinky die-cast No. 101 was a great replica of Thunderbird 2. It was manufactured in green (the correct colour) and for a reason known only to the people at Binns Road, in metallic blue as shown here. The battle-scarred example shown is from my own childhood collection and its condition testifies to its play-worthiness. Although it would be much more valuable mint and boxed, it still has its tiny Thunderbird 4, seen departing the open pod, and it gave me hours of fun. So in a deeply personal way I consider it more valuable than a boxed version that has never been played with.

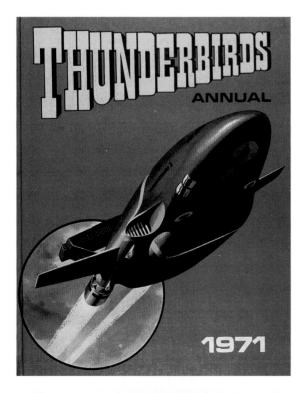

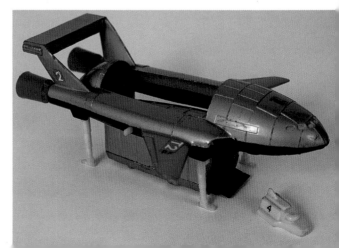

TV Classics Are Born

By the early 1970s, *Dad's Army*, first broadcast by the BBC in 1968, had become a comedy institution. Jimmy

Perry and David Croft's excellent scripts followed the antics of the Walmington-on-Sea Home Guard platoon as they braced themselves to meet Hitler's invading armies. Led by Captain Mainwaring, Lance-Corporal Jones, Sergeant Wilson, Privates Walker, Pike, Frazer and Godfrey and the local ARP Warden Bert Hodges combined to bring a combination of slapstick and pathos to every episode. As with all popular TV shows, publishers soon snapped up the rights to annuals – *Dad's Army*

LEFT: *Dad's Army* board game produced by Strawberry Fayre, a division of Denys Fisher in 1974.

BELOW LEFT: This *Dad's Army Annual* was bought for Simon Armstrong by his grandmother in 1973.

BELOW MIDDLE: *Dad's Army Annual 1976*. Introduced by wartime artiste Bud Flanagan singing 'Who do You Think You are Kidding, Mr Hitler?', a song written especially for the show by one of its writers, Jimmy Perry, *Dad's Army* was first broadcast in 1968. Jimmy Perry and David Croft's situation comedy about a Kentish Home Guard Unit during World War Two continued in production until 1977. Repeats of this marvellous programme have been more or less continually broadcast ever since.

BELOW RIGHT: *Dad's Army Annual 1978*. Although the series had ceased to be made a year previously, such was the popularity of the show that it still warranted an annual.

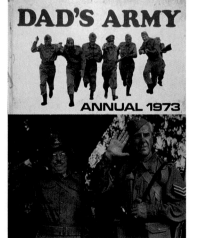

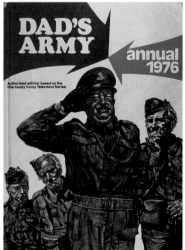

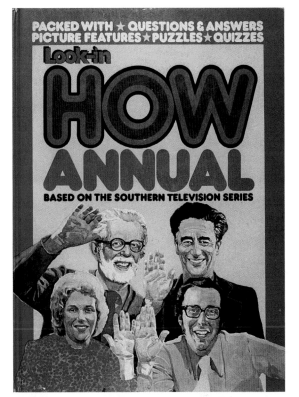

ABOVE: 'Based on the hilariously funny Television Series', *The Goodies Annual 1974*. Bill Oddie still regularly appears on BBC TV presenting nature programmes.

ABOVE: *How Annual* from 1975. The presenters of this classic Southern Television hands-on science show were Jon Miller, Bunty James, Fred Dinenage and the veteran Jack Hargreaves.

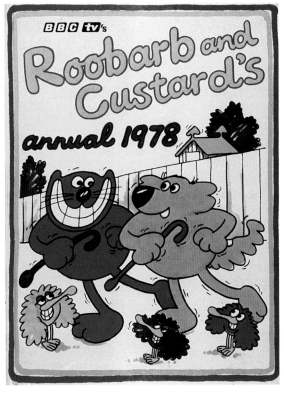

LEFT: With its distinctive sketchy style of animation, known in the business as 'boiling', Bob Godfrey's *Roobarb and Custard* first appeared on BBC TV in 1974. The annual shown dates from 1978. In 2003, British ITV Channel 5 bought the rights from Green Dog Films and from March that year brought Roobarb the dog and Custard the cat back to TV stardom.

Two versions of the phenomenally successful Stylophone from the early 1970s.

The Stylophone was a huge commercial success, up there with the Raleigh Chopper bicycle and Clackers, the hard plastic balls that children smashed together with a flick of the wrist (which part of a child's anatomy Clackers were also capable of smashing), and a variety of versions were manufactured. Boxed examples of the instrument are now very collectable. 'The Electronic Organ in Your Pocket', as the advertising strapline declared, was also behind the ethereal whines on David Bowie's hit 'Space Oddity', and subsequent appearances on recordings by bands such as Pulp have enhanced the Stylophone's legendary status.

The blurring of the traditional vocational divisions between popular musicians and TV celebrities was accentuated when David Cassidy, star of hit US TV show, *The Partridge Family* and every teenage girl's favourite pin-up in the early 1970s, began packing concert venues performing hits like 'I Think I Love You' and 'Breaking Up is Hard to Do'. Early Partridge family and

BELOW: **All good clean fun –** *The Partridge Family.*

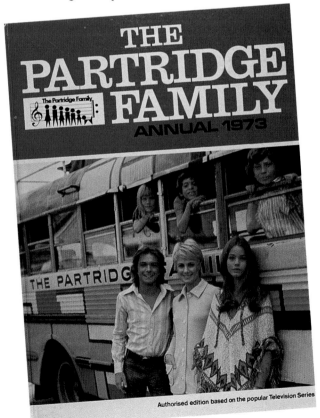

ones from the early and mid-1970s being particularly collectable.

Another enormously popular entertainer then as now is Rolf Harris. Painter and all-round entertainer Rolf had a hit single with 'Two Little Boys' the Christmas before Clive Dunn's hit, 'Granddad'. He also hosted a popular light entertainment show on BBC TV, dazzling audiences with his virtuosity with tins of paint and brushes that seemed more suitable for applying wallpaper paste.

At the time, Rolf Harris was equally famous for his connections with a hit instrument – the Stylophone. This was a pocket organ and electronic synthesizer, invented by Brian Jarvis, co-founder in 1967 of the British company Dubreq that marketed the product. Dubreq shrewdly hired Rolf Harris, a face familiar to millions of British TV viewers, to promote the product, which he did with his trademark enthusiasm and sincerity.

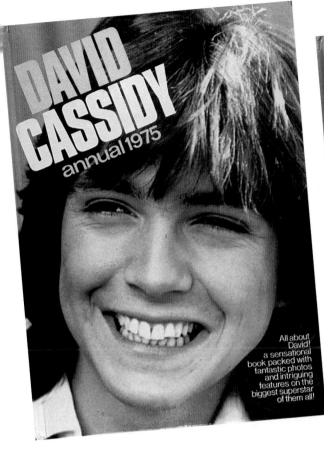

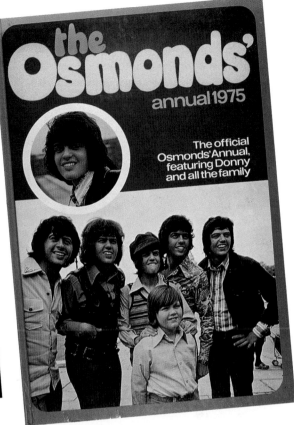

ABOVE: **By the mid-1970s David Cassidy was the pin-up of millions of pre-pubescent girls, their elder sisters and … their mothers.**

ABOVE RIGHT: *The Osmond's Annual 1975*. **Together with David Cassidy, the Osmond family was the US response to Britain's predilection for Glam Rock in the early 1970s.**

RIGHT: **'Shang-a-lang' – it's the Bay City Rollers. One of the biggest 'teeny bop' groups of all time, by the mid-1970s the five tartan-sporting Scottish lads had reached the height of their celebrity. This jigsaw puzzle is an example of one of the countless souvenirs available at the time.**

David Cassidy annuals and memorabilia are particularly collectable.

In 1973, manufacturer Invicta's portable *Mastermind* game won 'Toy of the Year'. It was also selected by the Design Centre London and awarded that organization's distinctive black and white chequered kitemark. Even this didn't reduce its sales! Unfortunately, the oil crisis of the same period did, as it resulted in less plastic being manufactured – bad news for a game that was flying off the shelves but was made of plastic.

RIGHT: *Angels Annual* from 1977. The popular BBC soap about nurses from Saint Angela's Hospital.

BELOW: This Angels doll and accessory set was one of a range of toys produced in 1977 by manufacturer Denys Fisher Toys under licence to the BBC. 'Now every trainee Angels nurse can have her very own ward and patient!'

Star Trek: The Seventies

Science fiction was as strong as ever in the 1970s and, as we shall see, almost defined the latter part of the decade with the films *Star Wars* and *Close Encounters of the Third Kind*. On the small screen, *Star Trek*'s enormous appeal continued to build and more kits and related toys were available in the 1970s than in the previous decade when the show first aired.

By the 1970s, the famous US Mego Corporation (founded in 1954) had entered the profitable action-figure market. The success of GI Joe, which had been launched by Hasbro in the USA in 1964, had proved that boys *would* play with dolls. Wanting to differentiate its product from the established 12in (305mm) figure market, Mego launched a series of 8in (203mm) figures. The first, Action Jackson, was released in 1972.

One of Mego's cleverest deals was securing the *Star Trek* merchandising licence in the early 1970s. At the time, although it had a legion of die-hard fans, *Star Trek* didn't rank too highly as a commercial property. Mego allegedly picked up the rights for a song. In 1974, Mego created a new range of 8in figures based on the crew of *Star Trek*'s *USS Enterprise* NCC-1701. These figures

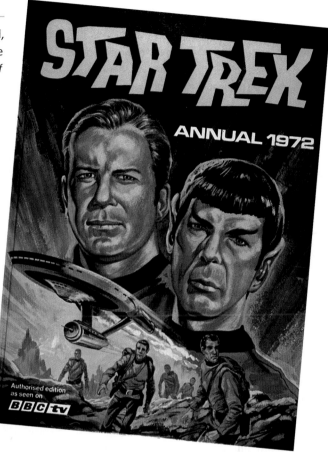

ABOVE: *Star Trek Annual 1972*.

Rare GAF Viewmaster presentation of *Star Trek* based on the original TV series. This twenty-one-view multi-disc and booklet set dates to 1968.

were actually inspired more by *Star Trek: The Animated Series*, which was based on the original TV programme, but 'drawn' by established US animation house, Filmation. The series of twenty-two animated episodes was aired from 1973–75 with reruns on NBS in 1975. Mego produced two distinct series of figures. All are now highly collectable, but the aliens in the range, the Romulans and Klingons, generally sell for the highest price.

In the mid-1970s, Mego supplemented its range of *Star Trek* toys with items such as communicators. American kids could talk to their friends and annoy passing truckers, intercepting their CB radio transmissions: 'Hello Rubber Duck. Ten-Four'… 'Hello, Scottie here!'

Other Mego toys included a *Star Trek* tricorder. This was really a standard audiotape cassette recorder dressed up with all sorts of gizmos and surface detail to look like Mr Spock's favourite hi-tech instrument.

Mego's 'Super Phaser II Target Game' came in a box emblazoned with both Kirk and Spock zapping space aliens. Inside was a very accurate replica of a phaser ray gun and a target depicting a Klingon Bird of Prey

spaceship. Nearly thirty years old, this toy is a fore-runner of the kind of laser tag games popular today.

Mego enjoyed a real boost when, in 1979, *Star Trek: The Motion Picture* was released. Directed by Robert Wise, editor of *Citizen Kane* for trivia buffs, the movie

ABOVE: **This wonderful Lone Star (British-made) 'Star Trek Inter-Space Communicator' is complete in its original packaging. It dates from 1974. 'Beam me up Scottie!'**

LEFT: **Whitman jigsaw puzzle showing Captain Kirk and Mr Spock narrowly escaping the attentions of a space monster due to the sharp shooting phaser operator on board the** *Enterprise.*

STAR TREK 224 LARGE PIECE PUZZLE

BBC tv

WHITMAN 7611

RIGHT: 'It's life Jim, but not as we know it.' Another evocative Whitman *Star Trek* puzzle from the early 1970s.

LEFT: **Mego 12in Captain Kirk doll from *Star Trek: The Motion Picture* released in 1979. Thousands of this and the other popular *Star Trek* figures in the range were sold. Sadly, relatively few survive today. If possible, collectors should try to find boxed versions, although such is their appeal that even loose figures have a value.**

not only revitalized the entire *Star Trek* concept, leading to a further eight cinematic sequels, it encouraged a fresh cadre of youngsters to purchase toys related to the film and original TV series.

Released at the same time as *Star Trek: The Motion Picture* premiered, Mego offered a range of larger 12in figures of the aging crew of the *Enterprise*. The script

involved all the usual suspects, but featured new characters Captain Decker and Lieutenant Ilia, the latter being replaced by a robotic probe sent to study the humans ('carbon units') aboard the *Enterprise* by 'V'ger' (the interplanetary probe Voyager). Consequently, Mego's 12in range included figures of Captain Kirk and Mr Spock but also newcomers like Ilia.

AMT kit of the original, and in this author's humble opinion, best Starship *Enterprise*, good old NCC-1701.

BELOW: US kit giant Aurora didn't have the US licence for *Star Trek* (rival AMT did). Instead, in the early 1970s the company used its UK subsidiary to manufacture this great diorama of Mr Spock battling a multi-headed serpent. Inquisitive Science Officer that he was, he clearly decided the best way of dealing with this alien was ... to shoot it.

Mint and boxed, these figures, which as all 'Trekkies' know, appeared at the rebirth of the famous franchise, are now very collectable.

Mego also produced a set of *Star Trek: The Motion Picture* wrist communicators, though they were not as successful as the Star Trek walkie-talkie versions released a few years earlier.

Many *Star Trek* construction kits date from the 1970s. American plastic kit manufacturer AMT, a company incorporated in 1948 as Aluminum Model Toys, had the licence to produce *Star Trek* kits in the US and produced its first model of the Starship *Enterprise* in 1966.

AMT chose only to produce spaceships, however. Not having the US licence, American competitor Aurora was forced to release its *Star Trek* kits from subsidiaries in the UK, initially releasing its replica of the *Enterprise* in 1968. You can tell it's a British kit because on the box it says 'As seen on BBC TV'.

Though tooled in the 1960s, Aurora's figure kit depicting Mr Spock battling a many-headed alien serpent was not released until 1972 and then it was only available in the UK because Aurora didn't want to have to pay the huge royalties required by rights owners

Desilu Studios and AMT. That same year, Aurora UK also released kits of the *Enterprise* and a Klingon cruiser.

One of the most collectable *Star Trek* toys is Dinky No. 358, a lovely die-cast metal and plastic replica of the original *Enterprise*. This was first produced in 1976

Dinky Toys catalogue No. 13 from 1977. The cover shows the USS *Enterprise* and a Klingon Battle Cruiser in battle (the Klingon ship has just fired its photon torpedo). Dinky produced a wonderful set of both spaceships (Dinky Toy No. 102).

BELOW: Marvellous Dinky Toy die-cast USS *Enterprise* from *Star Trek*. Not to be mistaken for mints, some of its unloaded photon torpedoes lie in the foreground.

and in the range until 1980. It fired little orange discs representing photon torpedoes. Boxed versions of this toy are rarely seen and are soon snapped up when they do become available.

In 1977 Dinky also produced a larger set featuring the USS *Enterprise*, together with a Klingon Battle Cruiser. Youngsters could now recreate the battles between Starfleet's finest and the aggressive Klingon Empire.

Doctor Who Travels On

In Britain, *Doctor Who* continued to be very popular. This was largely due to the appeal of the two actors playing the Doctor during the 1970s. They were John Pertwee, the third Doctor, who starred between 1970 and 1974, and the fourth Doctor, Tom Baker, who took over from Pertwee and made the role his own until 1981.

A wide range of licensed toy merchandise was produced in the 1970s. The most notable and today the most collectable items include two gems from British manufacturer Palitoy, which was based in Coalville in Leicestershire. In 1970 Palitoy manufactured a superb talking Dalek. Pre solid-state electronic memory storage, this toy contained a tiny magnetic disc with recordings on only one side of the platter. Consequently, although the Dalek uttered a variety of commands, including, of course, 'Exterminate!', its repertoire was somewhat limited. Hundreds of thousands were sold, but, being intended as playthings, naturally few survive intact. Boxed examples are highly prized. Unboxed examples

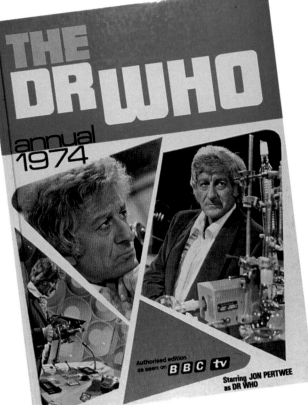

ABOVE: *Dr Who Annual 1974.*

LEFT: **Whitman *Dr. Who* puzzle, released in 1970 when actor Patrick Troughton passed the baton to new boy Jon Pertwee.**

of this wonderful toy are also of value, but be sure they are complete with miniature 'sink plungers', ray guns and eyepieces. These vulnerable attachments were the first things to be broken or lost.

Tom Baker is famous for his long scarf, floppy hat and general eccentricity. He is also famous for his pet dog – the robot K-9. In 1974, Palitoy followed the success of its talking Dalek with a talking K-9. This time, Palitoy

Dr Who jigsaw puzzle showing Jon Pertwee with his vintage car, 'Bessie'.

BELOW LEFT: *Terry Nation's Dalek Annual 1976*: 'E-X-T-E-R-M-I-N-A-T-E!'

BELOW RIGHT: 1970s battery-operated Talking Dalek. Boxed versions like this are hard to find now. Be sure that, boxed or loose, these toys are complete with all accessories. The Dalek's gun and sucker arm (sink plunger!) have a habit of becoming loose.

Dr Who and Bessie – his Edwardian roadster. 100 pieces. Jigsaw size approx. 11"x 9". By arrangement with BBCtv. Starring JON PERTWEE as the famous Dr Who.

Palitoy talking K-9 from the late 1970s. This 'loose' example works, but though harder to find and much more valuable, boxed versions are to be preferred, of course.

BELOW: In 1978 British manufacturer Denys Fisher produced a 10in figure of Tom Baker as Doctor Who. The version shown here is identical but produced by Italian manufacturer Harbert under licence from Denys Fisher.

provided a double-sided record and K-9 was capable of more phrases than the previous Dalek. Coming complete with a neat collar, rotating antennae (ears) and a bendy metal tail, a push of a button on the control panel on K-9's back would trigger one of a series of mechanical utterances such as 'Mission accomplished'.

Palitoy's K-9 replica is now quite rare; boxed examples with working audio features even more so. After an absence from TV screens (as a regular series) of twenty-four years, K-9 reappeared in an episode in 2005 with David Tennant as the tenth Doctor Who. This appearance naturally initiated nostalgic stirring amongst Who fans and, not surprisingly, increased the value of Palitoy's venerable old toy.

In 1978, British manufacturer Denys Fisher produced a 10in (254mm) figure of Tom Baker's Doctor Who incarnation. It came complete with hat, scarf and a tiny replica of the Doctor's sonic screwdriver. Italian manufacturer, Harbert, which was based in Milan, also produced this very popular figure under licence. The example shown in this book is one of Harbert's. Apart from the script on the box, it is identical in every way to the Denys Fisher version. For some reason, today there seem to be more 'Italian' Doctors around than British versions. I can only assume that a supply of factory fresh stock was unearthed on the continent in the 1990s.

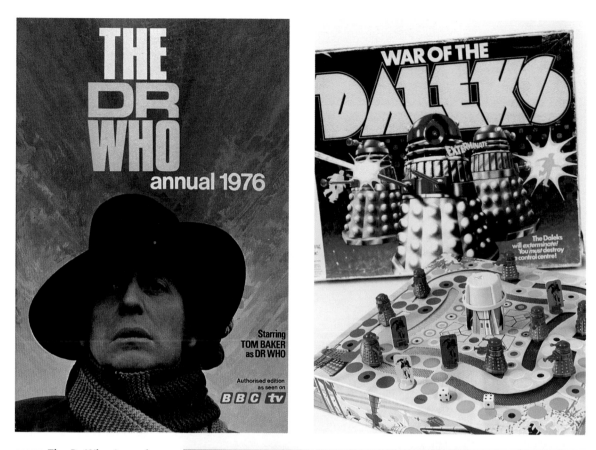

ABOVE: The *Dr Who Annual 1976* with K-9's master, as played by Tom Baker, on the cover.

ABOVE RIGHT: The 'War of the Daleks', a Denys Fisher board game from the 1970s.

RIGHT: 'Enemies of Doctor Who' jigsaw puzzle from 1976.

Created by Dalek creator Terry Nation, his new science-fiction adventure series, *Blake's 7*, was transmitted on BBC TV from January 1978 to December 1981. This vintage puzzle features the team's trusty spaceship, the *Liberator*.

BELOW: *Gerry Anderson's Space 1999 Annual* from 1977.

Authorised edition based on the popular Television Series

Denys Fisher also produced an action figure of Doctor Who's tribal warrior companion Leela as well as replicas of his time travelling TARDIS ('Time And Relative Dimensions In Space') and in 1976 one of the most collectable toys, a 10in (250mm) 'Giant Robot'. American companies Mego and Marx also produced a variety of *Doctor Who* toys in the 1970s.

Space: 1999

Another British science-fiction classic from the early to mid-1970s was Gerry Anderson's *Space: 1999*. This, a direct development of what was going to be the next instalment of Anderson's *UFO* concept, but which, due to poor ratings in the USA, was not recommissioned, ran for forty-eight episodes between 1973–76. Set on a base ('Alpha') on the Moon, which had been knocked out of orbit due to a nuclear explosion, each fifty-minute episode was full of the fantastic vehicles and spaceships Anderson fans had come to expect.

Probably the most collectable toys associated with the series are those manufactured by Dinky. The British manufacturer produced high-quality die-casts of both the Eagle Transporter and Eagle Freighter spaceships from the series. Both of these toys are very collectable, mint and boxed versions being more so, of course. The Transporter was finished in green; the blue-coloured Freighter was more or less identical, except that in place of a cargo container it was underslung with drums of 'radioactive' waste. These are often missing from loose examples of this vessel. Lucky owners of boxed variants should ensure they have all the correct decals intact, especially the sticky ones that came separately with the Freighter and were designed to be applied to the toxic cargo. These are often missing.

British plastic construction kit manufacturer Airfix had obtained the licence to produce model kits of the vehicles in *Space: 1999*. The company's 1970s releases of an Eagle Transporter and Hawk spaceship, both featuring each vessel's distinctive bird-like nose sections, are extremely hard to find unassembled and in their original boxes.

Mint and boxed Dinky Toys No. 359 die-cast replica of the Eagle Transporter from *Space 1999*. Mint and boxed examples of any of Gerry Anderson's creations sell for premium prices; this toy, dating from 1976–77, is also complete with its very vulnerable expanded polystyrene insert ('the lunar surface').

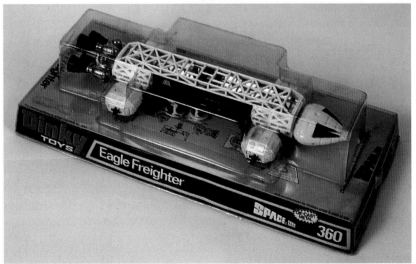

Sister craft to the *Space 1999* Eagle Transporter was the Eagle Freighter. Equally rare, before purchasing one (ideally in its box or later vacuum-formed blister pack like the one shown here), collectors should ensure that the vehicle's 'radioactive waste' canisters are attached and complete with their adhesive decals.

ABOVE LEFT: **Airfix Hawk spaceship from *Space 1999*.**

ABOVE: **Captain Zantor 6in figure – a more recent replica of a vintage item from the 1970s series.**

Space 1999 **jigsaw puzzle manufactured in 1974.**

Merchandising Defined: *Star Wars*

Viewing audiences had developed an appetite for science fantasy and this was reinforced with the success of *Close Encounters of the Third Kind* in 1977. However, when mentioning the phrases 'science fiction' and 'toy merchandise' in the same breath as 'the 1970s', one can't avoid the film that redefined the genre: *Star Wars*.

As everyone knows, the *Star Wars* series now totals six blockbusting epics, with the first three films – *Star*

Wars, *The Empire Strikes Back* and *Return of the Jedi* – actually being made and released years before the most recent trio explaining the origins of the saga and the antecedents of famous characters like Darth Vader and Luke Skywalker.

Long a dream of George Lucas, fresh from the success of *American Graffiti*, the award-winning film about the life of US teenagers in the 1950s that he wrote and directed, perhaps he alone saw *Star Wars*' real potential. Certainly, studio 20th Century Fox, which picked up the film after most others had turned it down, saw

ABOVE: **Could you escape the Death Star in the late 1970s with this classic *Star Wars* board game manufactured by Britain's Palitoy?**

Star Wars Annual No. 1, **published by Grandreams in 1978.**

little merit in it and was allegedly preparing to hive off its investment in the property as a tax shelter.

It's certainly true that George Lucas waived the normal writer/director's fee in exchange for a payment of $175,000 and 40 per cent of the merchandising rights. Seeing little value in this area, studio executives readily agreed to his terms. Even Kenner Toys, which only signed a toy-merchandising contract shortly before the film premiered, wasn't convinced related toys would sell in great numbers.

In the event, the 1977 film was an enormous commercial success, breaking all box-office records and winning seven Academy awards, thereby vindicating Lucas's faith in the project. Kenner was overwhelmed by the demand and was forced to resort to providing vouchers in exchange for toys when they became available. Alone, the merchandising rights generated so much income for Lucas that he has been financially independent of the studio system ever since.

Vintage *Star Wars* toys are some of the most collectable there have ever been. The range of action figures, vehicles, light sabres, games, diecasts and model kits available is massive and capable of filling a very thick book by itself. However, it's worth highlighting some classic pieces and pointing out specific features of interest to the collector.

Perhaps the most significant thing about *Star Wars* toys is the availability of hundreds of 3in (76mm) figures associated with the various chapters of the saga. Until *Star Wars*, action figures were either of the traditional Action Man/GI Joe 12in (300mm) tall variety or perhaps of a similar composition but only 8in (200mm) or 10in (250mm) tall. *Star Wars* toys included a large selection of the various spacecraft in the film: the *Millennium Falcon*, TIE (Twin Ion Engine) Fighters, Snowspeeders and the like. These vehicles were designed to accommodate the relevant action figure pilots and crew, ensuring maximum play value from the range. To keep these toys to within reasonable dimensions, it was decided that the figures for them should be no larger than 3in. Despite this, however, Palitoy's *Falcon*, released in 1977, was a large beast and a highly prized toy.

The initial *Star Wars* figures range totalled only twelve carded figures. Each figure was presented inside a clear plastic, vacuum-formed blister attached to a stiff card – hence the term 'carded'. On the back of each card were details of the twelve figures then available. Consequently, collectors know them as 'twelve backs'. The range was quickly extended, growing to sets of twenty and twenty-one. The twenty-first figure was a miniature of bounty hunter Boba Fett. These early figures are highly prized, especially the replica of Boba, which is worth the most.

Larger-sized 12in action figures, complete with detachable garments and more highly detailed accessories, were also produced by Kenner, between the years 1979 and 1980.

Classic 1970s Kenner TIE Fighter containing a tiny replica of the evil Darth Vader.

Examples of toys from the first series and branded 'Star Wars' are naturally the rarest, with mint and boxed items commanding the highest prices. Palitoy produced many of these. Its replica of a Landspeeder, released in 1978, and its *Star Wars* Cantina Playset from the following year are particularly collectable.

Most of the *Star Wars* model kits were produced in association with the later movies, *The Empire Strikes Back* (1980) and *Return of the Jedi* (1983). An early and very collectable kit, however, is Denys Fisher's 6in (152mm) tall replica of R2-D2 ('Artoo-Detoo') available in 1978.

US kit manufacturer MPC was also an early manufacturer of *Star Wars* replicas. In 1977 it manufactured a 1/72 scale kit (over 18in/457mm long) of Han Solo's *Millennium Falcon*, as well as an excellent 1/10 scale R2-D2. The following year, it released a superb 1/48 scale kit of Darth Vader's TIE Fighter and a replica of 'The authentic Luke Skywalker's X-Wing Fighter' in the same scale.

Star Wars board games were also very popular. Parker got its version, 'Adventures of R2-D2', into the shops in 1977, with Kenner releasing its 'Escape from the Death Star' in 1979.

The success of *Star Wars* naturally encouraged the studios to produce science fiction – it seemed the public had a real appetite for it.

A very rare French Meccano
Z-6PO (similar sounding in
French to C-3PO) from 1977
and, from the same year,
a Denys Fisher kit of the
robot's pal, R2-D2.

**Climbing Batman figure manufactured by
Ideal in the late 1970s.**

Further Film and TV Spin-Offs

When Universal Studios released *Battlestar Galactica* in 1978, the year following the release of *Star Wars*, it was sued by 20th Century Fox for copyright infringement, with Fox arguing that *Battlestar Galactica* had stolen over thirty ideas from *Star Wars*. Universal counter-sued, claiming *Star Wars* had borrowed much from the Buck Rogers serials of the 1940s and that R2-D2 and C-3PO mimicked the robots Huey, Dewey and Louie from Douglas Trumbull's 1971 sci-fi movie *Silent Running*. The lawsuit was dismissed in 1980.

Unaware of the behind-the-scenes in-fighting in Hollywood, audiences enjoyed the two-hour-long movie *Battlestar Galactica* and the TV series that followed. Both film and series starred Lorne Green as Commander Adama in charge of the *Galactica*, the only Colonial military vessel to have survived an attack by the cybernetic Cylons.

A variety of toys in association with both the movie and the TV series were released. Mattel produced a large range of carded figures made to a similar 3in size to that pioneered by *Star Wars*. The firm also manufactured a range of vehicles including Colonial Vipers,

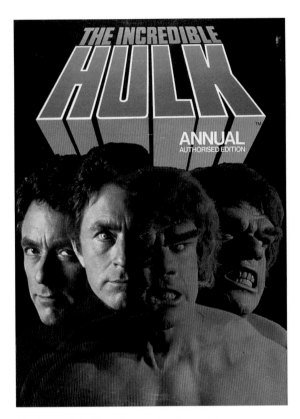

The Incredible Hulk Annual 1979, published by Marvel Comics. The cover shows the metamorphosis of the actor Bill Bixby into Lou Ferrigno's Hulk. How many other viewers wondered, like I did, exactly what happened to all the torn clothes?

Kung Fu was enormously popular in the early 1970s. Influential, too, as the number of youngsters being rushed into A&E departments of local hospitals with a variety of broken and twisted limbs testified. This *Kung Fu Annual* dates from 1975.

Cylon Raiders and the missile-armed tracked Colonial Landram. Mattel also produced larger action figures, its boxed Cylon Centurion being particularly handsome.

US manufacturer Monogram had secured the licence to produce construction kits from *Battlestar Galactica* and in 1978 it first released a 1/24 scale Colonial Viper linked to the film and later that year released it again, but this time classified Space Fighter Viper, together with a Space Fighter Raider (Cylon Raider), and associated with the TV series. Moulded in 1/24 scale, each of the kits was of a substantial size. They are all very collectable, although only if they are unmade and complete with decals and instructions.

Released in 1979, Walt Disney's *The Black Hole* was another sci-fi movie that spawned a selection of toy and model spin-offs. A range of carded figures of the robots, Maximillian and VINCENT ('Vital Information Necessary, Centralized'), the stars of the film, were available. However, some of the most rare items are MPC's 1/12 scale construction kits of the duo. Maximillian stood over 11in (279mm) tall and was moulded in two colours and came complete with a stand; VINCENT was a respectable 9in (229mm) tall.

The final major sci-fi TV series of the 1970s was *Buck Rogers in the 25th Century*, a fresh treatment of the 1930s classic starring Gil Gerard as Capt William 'Buck' Rogers and Erin Gray in the role of Wilma Deering. Between 1979 and 1981, there were thirty-seven hour-long episodes of the popular action series, following the adventures of an astronaut who is revived

A clockwork walking
V.I.N.CENT toy from Disney's
1979 movie *The Black Hole*.
It was manufactured in Hong
Kong for Louis Marx and
Company Ltd.

BELOW: A carded Mego
Sentry Robot from
The Black Hole (1979).

after being in suspended animation for 500 years and
becomes the Earth's champion.

Buck Rogers annuals, kits (Monogram made a particularly good 1/48 scale version of a Marauder from the
show) and even a Corgi die-cast of the hero's starfighter were produced in association with the show. My
favourites, however, have to be Mego's 12in action
figures. Their likeness of Buck is good, but for impact
and rarity, their 12in version of Tiger Man takes some
beating. As with all Mego figures from the 1970s,
boxed examples are very rare. Also, like many such figures (*Star Trek* and so on) the faces of the *Buck Rogers*
characters tend to discolour with age, clearly being

LEFT: This Corgi replica of the starfighter from *Buck
Rogers in the 25th Century* was produced in 1981.
The wings operated, moving in and out with ease.

manufactured from a plastic different to that used for the rest of the body.

Whilst sticking with the 1970s TV science-fiction theme one can't avoid mentioning *The Six Million Dollar Man* and *The Bionic Woman*, two hugely popular TV shows that generated an enormous amount of licensed toys and other merchandise.

Running from 1974–78, *The Six Million Dollar Man* starred Lee Majors as test pilot Steve Austin. Following a near fatal crash, the powers that be decide that they have 'the power to rebuild him'. The crippled Austin is reassembled with a variety of cybernetic body parts that convey superhuman powers. But as the rebuild cost six

LEFT: **Rare Denys Fisher Col Steve Austin 12in action figure from 1975. Looking though his 'bionic' eye conferred superhuman powers on children. Surviving examples of this toy, complete with the individual engine block that the Colonel could so easily lift, are most desirable.**

BELOW: **Denys Fisher's 'Bionic Crisis' game, based on the hugely popular *Six Million Dollar Man* series, was manufactured in 1976.**

million dollars, he is encouraged to work as a special agent for the 'Office of Scientific Investigation' to repay his debt to the government. The rest is history.

In 1976, halfway through *The Six Million Dollar Man*'s run, actress Lindsay Wagner assumed the role of Jaime Sommers, a professional tennis player who suffers a near fatal parachute accident and is saved by special bionic surgery. Like Steve Austin, Jaime Sommers joins the OSI and begins an equal career as a superhuman crime fighter.

The most collectable toys associated with both *The Six Million Dollar Man* and *The Bionic Woman* are the Denys Fisher figures of Sommers and Austin that were made under licence from Kenner. In fact, Kenner in the USA and Denys Fisher in Britain released a wide range of accessories for their 12in figures. The 'Bionic Transport and Repair Station' released in 1975 is particularly sought after, as are the figures of Oscar Goldman (Steve Austin's boss) and Steve's nemesis, Maskatron. The Kenner Bionic Bigfoot figure – 'the Sasquatch beast' – looked rather like Radio One DJ Dave Lee Travis circa 1980 and was scaled to tower over Steve.

American fans had far more product to choose from than those of us on this side of the Atlantic, for example items such as Kenner's OSI Headquarters, showing the hi-tech interior of Oscar Goldman's office with room for a couple of action figures to lounge against the desk, or wall-mounted video consoles adjacent to a furled Stars and Stripes banner.

ABOVE: **1975 Denys Fisher's** *The Bionic Woman* **game.**

RIGHT: **Not satisfied with one Bionic Man board game, Denys Fisher produced two. In this one, 'Steve Austin rescues stranded astronauts ... prevents a nuclear blackmail attempt ... knocks out an international crime ring and ... locates an underwater missile network.' All in a day's work for the Six Million Dollar Man!**

'Bionic Repair', a snap-together MPC kit from US giant General Mills' Fundimensions division, shows Bionic Woman Jaime Sommers and her mentor Oscar Goldman busily repairing her hi-tech structure.

RIGHT: Denys Fisher made the most of its *Six Million Dollar Man* concession – this snap-together kit of Col Austin casually grappling with an ape the size of King Kong is another collectable classic from the company's stable.

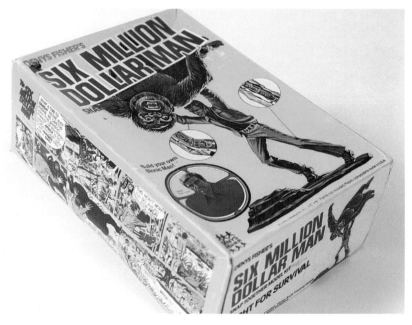

Fortunately, MPC's snap-together Bionic Repair Lab, featuring a benign Oscar Goldman whipping open the Bionic Woman's shin and making a quick repair, as Jaime Sommers lies on the operating table and helpfully passes him a pair of pliers, was available in the UK. Also available was the Denys Fisher kit of Steve Austin performing a very neat judo throw on a giant gorilla.

In 1973, a year before his big break playing the Bionic Man, Lee Majors had married Texan actress and model, Farrah Fawcett. Like 'Posh and Becks' several decades later, in the mid-1970s Lee and Farrah Fawcet-Majors, as she was now called, rarely escaped the media spotlight. A stunning photograph of Farrah in a swimsuit quickly became one of the bestselling posters of all time, convincing Hollywood of her celebrity.

Post Farrah Fawcett-Majors, the new *Charlie's Angels* line-up grace this jigsaw puzzle manufactured by SPP in 1978.

BELOW: *Charlie's Angels Annual 1979.* In 1975, the classic all-girl crime-fighting trio of Jill, Sabrina and Kelly first burst onto our screens in Spelling and Goldberg's hugely successful TV series.

Consequently, in 1975 legendary producers Aaron Spelling and Leonard Goldberg asked Farrah to star with Kate Jackson and Jaclyn Smith in a new production, *Charlie's Angels.* Farrah played Jill, with Jackson and Smith, respectively, as Sabrina and Kelly. The show was a huge success and merchandised product poured forth. Popular with children as well as adults, *Charlie's Angels* encouraged toy manufacturers to snap up licences for dolls, action figures, cosmetic outfits, games, jigsaw puzzles and even plastic kits. American toy brands Hasbro and Mego led the way with a wide range of items.

Hasbro released a range of 8.5in (216mm) dolls of each of the Angels, which could also be purchased in sets of three. Two different sets were available, one featuring Farrah's replacement, Cheryl Ladd (Farrah ceased being a full-time member of the cast after only a year), who played Jill Monroe's younger sister, Kris. By 1977 Hasbro had provided its dolls with a wide variety of outfits and accessories. Presented in distinctive blister packs, there were twelve different outfits for youngsters to choose from.

The same year, Mego released larger 12in versions of Farrah Fawcett-Majors and Jaclyn Smith. These came in quite separate packaging styles. The Farrah doll was in a green window box, with the figure clad in a white catsuit and sporting Farrah's distinctive hairstyle, a flicked-back look that helped to push hairdressers' profits through the roof in 1976–77. The Farrah doll was also produced under licence to Mego in Britain by Airfix.

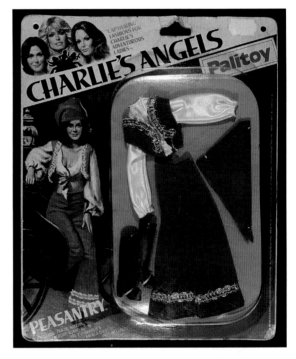

LEFT: US manufacturer Hasbro produced a range of 8.5in dolls of each of the Angels. The doll shown is of Jill, Farah Fawcett-Majors' character. It came with a 'Twist 'n' turn waist and rooted hair you can style'.

ABOVE: This *Charlie's Angels* 'Peasantry' outfit was manufactured under licence by Palitoy in 1977. One in a series of 'Captivating fashions for Charlie's adventurous ladies', it was made to fit the 8.5in dolls already available.

LEFT: Hasbro-produced luxurious 'Golden Intrigue' outfit for one of the *Charlie's Angels'* dolls. It was one of Hasbro's 'Gold Coast Editions' and was manufactured in 1977.

Being somewhat more rare, the Airfix doll is now highly collectable.

Although Airfix released an action figure associated to the programme, US construction kit manufacturer Revell actually produced a model kit in 1977 – a 1/25 scale replica of the *Charlie's Angels* Mobile Unit Van. This featured the girls' distinctive decal, depicting them in silhouette wielding weapons and preparing to deliver lethal karate chops. The van was also available in the 1970s as a Corgi die-cast. Many of these items, although not the early dolls and kits, were re-released when the series was transformed into two blockbusting movies in 2000 and 2003, starring the new line-up of Cameron Diaz, Lucy Liu and Drew Barrymore.

Mork & Mindy, the hugely popular series about an alien, Mork from the planet Ork, played by Robin Williams, who arrives on Earth to study humans and their way of life, ran for ninety-four episodes between 1978 and 1982. With his famous greeting of 'Na-Nu-Na-Nu', Mork would get up to all sorts of zany antics, exasperating his flatmate 'Mindy' (Pam Dawber).

A huge array of toys, games and annuals were produced in association with *Mork & Mindy*. Action figures are some of the most collectable vintage TV toys around and in 1979 two particularly nice ones were produced by US manufacturer Mattel. Mattel's Mork doll came with a 'talking space pack' and was cleverly presented standing upside-down in its packaging. The Mindy doll was smaller and less popular. Mattel also produced a very collectable carded toy featuring the egg in which Mork arrived on Earth, containing a miniature representation of a spacesuit-clad Mork.

Mork was actually a spin-off from another internationally popular American TV series, *Happy Days* – in one episode of *Happy Days*, arriving from his home planet, Mork attempts to abduct Richie Cunningham to take him back to Ork as an example of a mundane human being. He is foiled by the super-cool Fonzie (Henry Winkler). *Happy Days* began life in 1974 and continued in one guise or another for ten years. No mean feat for any TV sitcom.

ABOVE: **In 1977 Mego released 12in versions of Farrah Fawcett-Majors and Jaclyn Smith. These were presented in two distinct packaging styles. The Farrah doll was also produced under licence from Mego by Airfix in Britain. Being somewhat more rare, the Airfix doll is now highly collectable.**

RIGHT: **Revell 1/25 scale replica of the *Charlie's Angels* Mobile Unit Van manufactured in 1977.**

LEFT: This *Mork & Mindy Annual* dates from 1981.

BELOW: In 1979 Mattel produced a range of 9in character dolls from *Mork & Mindy*. Mork is a loose figure, ready for youngsters to play with him, mimicking his catchphrases of 'Na-Nu-Na-Nu' and 'Shazbut'. The boxed doll is of Pam Dawber, the actress who played Mindy in the sitcom.

Being somewhat older than *Mork & Mindy*, surviving *Happy Days* toys are even harder to find. Probably the hardest items to source these days are the series of 8in dolls produced by Mego in 1976. Mego produced really good replicas of Fonzie, Richie, Ralph and Potsie. The figure of the Fonz, the icon of the show and an example of 'cool' to a generation, was clad in his trademark leather biker jacket.

Other hit American shows of the period with a range of supporting toy merchandise, especially games and die-cast vehicles, include *Starsky and Hutch*, *The Dukes of Hazzard* and *Kojak*. British manufacturer Corgi produced vehicles licensed to each of the shows.

On TV, *The Dukes of Hazzard* entertained millions between 1979 and 1985. US toy giant Mego produced a range of associated toys, including a selection of figures of each of the principal characters. Each figure was just short of 4in. They are all very collectable. Intact carded figures like this one of Luke Duke are highly collectable, loose figures less so.

RIGHT: Taiwanese manufacturer Unisonic produced these *Dukes of Hazzard* LCD calculators bearing branding from the hit TV series.

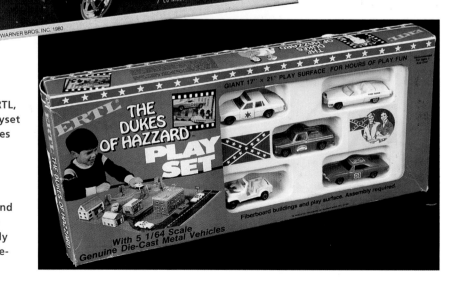

LEFT: A 1/25 scale plastic construction kit of Daisy's Jeep CJ, manufactured by US kit firm MPC.

RIGHT: Manufactured by ERTL, this *Dukes of Hazzard* Playset features a range of vehicles from the TV show. 'Easily assembled ... the Playset includes a realistic base, courthouse, garage, farmhouse, bridge, sign and trees.' It is now a sought-after collectable, especially with those who favour die-cast vehicles.

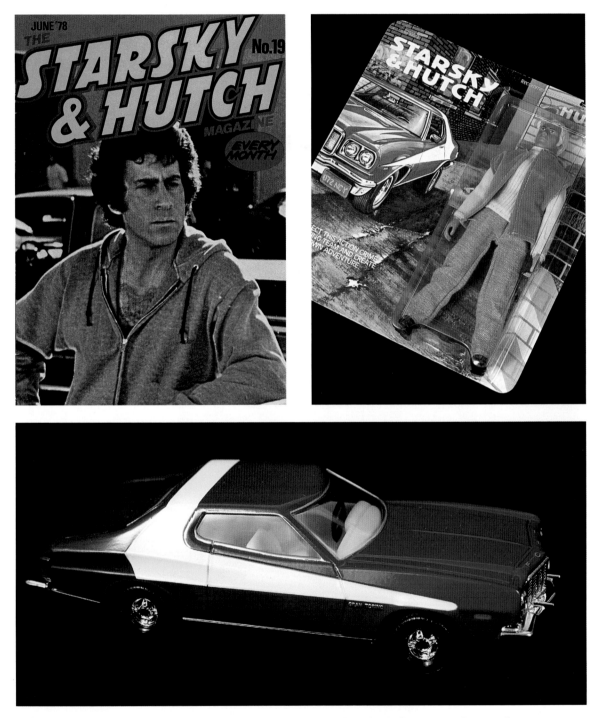

TOP LEFT: *Starsky & Hutch Magazine* from June 1978 featuring Paul Michael Glazer – Starsky – on the cover.

TOP RIGHT: Mego Hutch character doll from the 1970s.

ABOVE: Corgi's die-cast replica of Starsky's distinctive Gran Torino.

BELOW: *Kojak*, starring the inimitable Telly Savalas, was made between 1973–78. This *Kojak Book and Record Set* ('It's fun to read as you hear') dates from 1977.

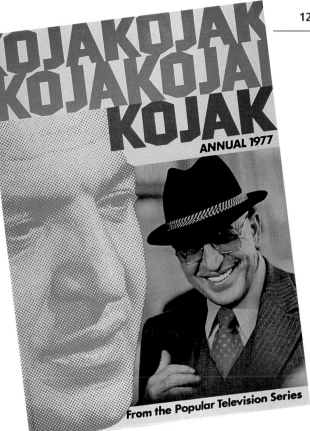

RIGHT: This classic *Kojak Annual* dates from 1977. Not long ago, you could pick these up for pennies at boot sales and in charity shops. With the recent growth in retro collectables, such items are becoming more and more pricey.

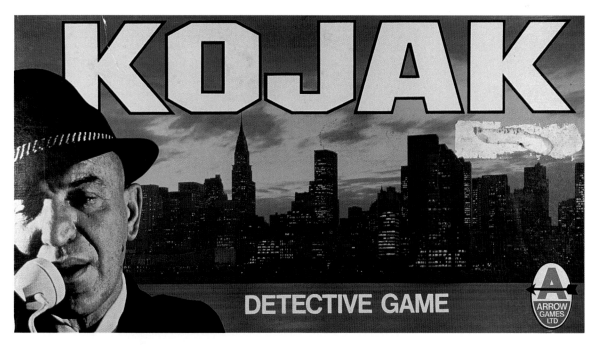

Naturally, the *Kojak* franchise was supported by board games like this mid-1970s one from Britain's Arrow Games.

Popular British TV series, other than good old *Dad's Army*, generated a range of home-produced toys too. There were games associated with *George and Mildred*, *On the Buses*, *Are You Being Served*, *The Golden Shot*, *It's a Knockout*, *New Faces* and even the incredibly pedestrian soap opera about a highway motel in the midlands, *Crossroads*.

Manufactured by Denys Fisher, the 'George v Mildred Dice Game' was licensed from the popular TV series of the same name produced between 1976–79.

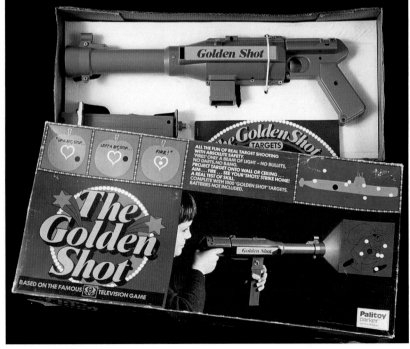

The Golden Shot target game, based on the famous British TV show that was first broadcast in 1967 but is best remembered when it was hosted by Bob Monkhouse in the early 1970s. His, and the show's, catchphrase became 'Bernie, the Bolt!' No danger of anyone being hurt by errant bolts with this Palitoy game manufactured in 1975. 'All the fun of real target shooting with absolute safety', promised the box.

BELOW: In the mid-1970s, British manufacturer Palitoy produced
the 'New Faces Game' – 'The laugh-a-minute showbiz game'
based on the hugely popular Independent Television talent show.

BELOW LEFT: Starring Reg Varney
as Stanley Butler, Bob Grant as
Jack, Anna Karen as Olive and
Stephen Lewis as Inspector
Cyril Blake ('I'll get you,
Butler!'), *On the Buses* was
on British TV from 1969 until
1973. The series spawned
three films by Britain's
Hammer Films: *On the Buses*
(1971), *Mutiny on the Buses*
(1972) and *Holiday on the
Buses* (1973). It also inspired
this board game manufactured
by Denys Fisher in 1973.

BELOW: *The David Nixon Show*
was on British TV between
1972–77. Before Paul Daniels
there was David Nixon.

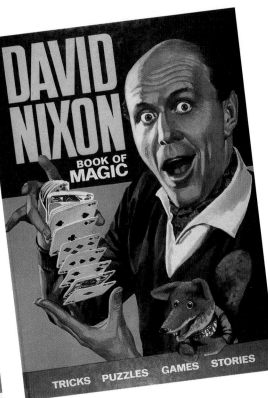

Delta Pastimes manufactured 'The Crossroads Motel' board game in 1977. 'A skilful and exciting game of hotel management for up to 4 players,' promised the box. In the 1970s it was interesting to discover which of your schoolmates played the *Colditz* board game and which played the *Crossroads* one. Those who played the latter probably had less fun, but I bet they are enjoying better careers now.

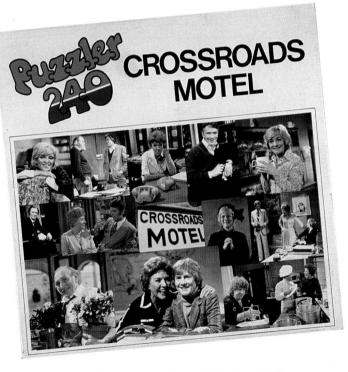

The Official Crossroads Special from 1982. 'Inside! Win a day at Crossroads'. Lucky winners might get the chance to meet Amy Turtle, Benny, Sandy Richardson, Meg Mortimer (Noele Gordon), Mr Lovejoy, Vince Parker, Jill Harvey or Adam Chance!

'Crossroads Motel' puzzle from 1978. This British soap, set in a motorway motel, was first transmitted in 1972. For a while in 1977 it was Britain's No. 1 TV show. The original series ended in 1988. It was revived in 2001 but because of dismal ratings lasted for only another couple of years before finally being axed for good in May 2003.

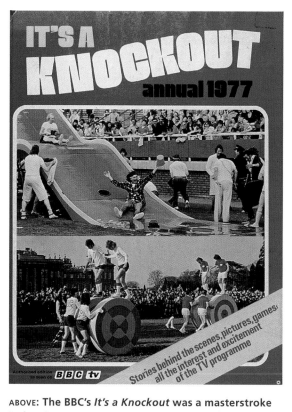

ABOVE: The BBC's *It's a Knockout* was a masterstroke in family viewing during its heyday in the 1970s. Presenters Stuart Hall and Eddie Waring proved the perfect choices to host this unselfconsciously kitsch show.

More serious and exciting fare included the BBC TV drama series *Colditz* (1972–74), the story of the infamous World War Two maximum-security POW camp, Oflag IV-C, and the struggles of Allied prisoners to escape its castellated fortifications. The show was enormously popular. *Colditz* was an ideal premise for games manufacturers and many were produced. Taking their turn, players representing *Colditz* prisoners had to outwit the camp guards and attempt successful escapes.

Though they were liberated before they bravely needed to resort to using it, the ingenious prisoners had actually manufactured and concealed a full-size glider in the castle's loft. Seizing on the marketing opportunity, Airfix produced a flying replica of the original machine.

ABOVE and LEFT: The BBC TV drama series *Colditz* (1972–74) was enormously popular and was the catalyst for various licensed products. British game manufacturer Parker realized the obvious potential for a board game based around the various escape attempts and the guards' efforts to thwart them.

LEFT: This is a very rarely seen 'catalogue rough' produced by kit manufacturer Airfix. It was used in the pre-publicity for the company's forthcoming flying model of the legendary 'Colditz glider'. It shows allied POWs in one of Colditz Castle's attics, building the aircraft from scrap material ...

RIGHT: ... and here's the one that Airfix built. It had an 18in wingspan and could be made to fly, which is more than can be said of the original glider, as Colditz was liberated before the prisoners were able to effect their escape. This Airfix product dates from 1974.

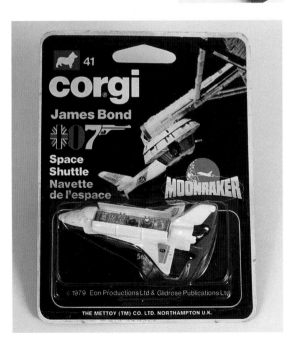

LEFT: Miniature Corgi 007 Moonraker space shuttle from 1979, complete in its original blister packaging.

Branded to tie in with the BBC series, the replica possessed an 18in (457mm) wingspan and came complete with a facsimile of the original plans. Because it was designed to be launched skywards and had to be of lightweight construction if it was to get airborne, few, if any, of the assembled Airfix *Colditz* gliders survive. Those that do and are complete with their packaging and instructions are highly prized.

Other hit British TV drama of the period include *The Sweeney* and *Minder* and they too were licensed to toy manufacturers that produced a range of games and branded merchandise.

The above is naturally only a selection of those movies and TV highlights that influenced toy manufacturers in the 1970s. I apologize for any omissions – it's a personal choice.

Of the other hit movies of the 1970s, three blockbusting movies, *Jaws* released in 1975, *Superman* from 1978 and the two Roger Moore Bond films from that period (*The Spy Who Loved Me* in 1977 and *Moonraker* from 1979), naturally had most impact on the motivations of toy manufacturers at the time.

Produced in the wake of *Jaws'* enormous appeal, US manufacturer Ideal gave fans 'The Game of Jaws' in 1976. Featuring a large polystyrene moulding of an enormous shark head in whose mouth were lodged pieces of debris from various attacks, players had to delicately remove bones, boots and coils of rope without triggering the loaded mechanism causing the fish's jaws to snap! This game, a kind of malign version of that old favourite, *Buckaroo*, was very popular with children. Consequently, a fair number of them turn up at car boot sales and toy fairs. The toy remained in production for quite some time because *Jaws 2*, the sequel to

the original film, was in the cinemas by 1978. Boxed versions complete with all the items are much more difficult to locate.

RIGHT: **'The Game of Jaws' was manufactured under licence by the Ideal Toy Co. Ltd in 1976. The Universal Pictures smash hit of the previous year had caused a sensation. Playing this game, which involved trying to hook items from the shark's mouth before its jaws snapped shut, was somewhat safer than tackling a Great White at sea.**

Revell GB kit from the late 1970s of oceanographer and TV personality Jacques Cousteau's ship, *Calypso*.
It was extremely finely detailed and even featured a miniature helicopter.

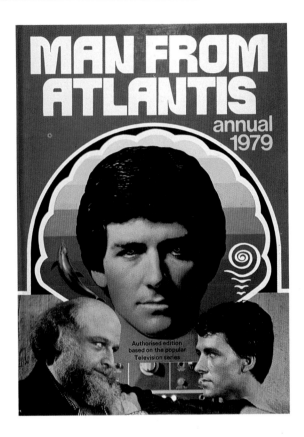

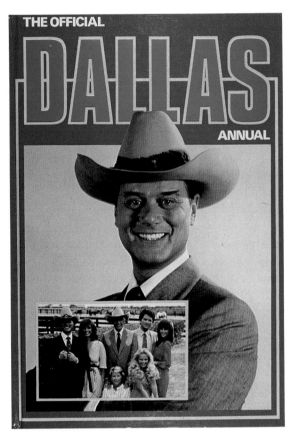

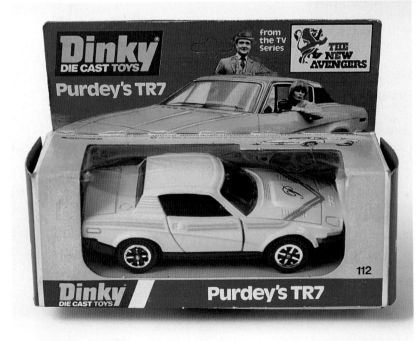

ABOVE LEFT: **From its beginnings in 1977, US television's** *Man From Atlantis*, **starring Patrick Duffy, was a hit on both sides of the Atlantic. This annual dates from 1979.**

ABOVE RIGHT: **Patrick Duffy turned up again in US blockbuster** *Dallas*, **which began life in 1978. This time, however, Duffy wasn't playing a naturally amphibious man, but J.R. Ewing's younger brother, Bobby.**

Purdey's TR7 from *The New Avengers* **TV series – Dinky Toy No. 112 from 1978.**

RETURN OF

THE SAINT

Annual 1979

Based on the popular television series
featuring Ian Ogilvy

The two Bond films were popular with young audiences because of two very different vehicles. James Bond drove another especially adapted vehicle in *The Spy Who Loved Me*. A lovely die-cast version of the car, a Lotus Esprit capable of converting to an amphibious and even underwater mode and which fired little red missiles, was produced by Corgi to coincide with the movie's launch.

Apart from Roger Moore, of course, the star of *Moonraker* was the space shuttle, then one of NASA's newest projects. Die-casts, plastic kits by Airfix and Revell in differing scales and a range of plastic toys were manufactured to represent the vehicle used by evil megalomaniac Hugo Drax to point a powerful laser at Earth.

Ridley Scott's *Alien* was one of the last big movies of the 1970s. Released in 1979, the story of the crew of a deep-space mining ship rerouted to answer an apparent SOS raised the sci-fi movie bar even higher.

When the crew of the *Nostromo* touch down on a distant planet to investigate, they discover that the 'SOS' was actually a warning. The *Nostromo* crew, which featured Sigourney Weaver as Ripley in the starring role she would reprise for another three blockbuster movies

ABOVE: The *Return of the Saint* starred actor Ian Ogilvy. This annual dates from 1979.

RIGHT: In 1979 US manufacturer Revell's British subsidiary produced this 1/25 scale snap-together construction kit of the Saint's Jaguar XJS.

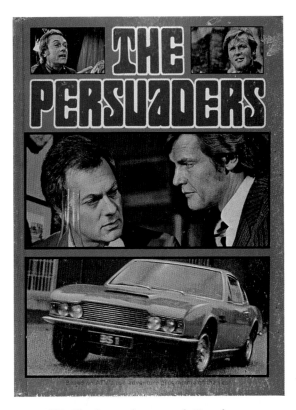

From 1972, *The Persuaders* annual, 'Based on ATV's top adventure programme of the year', was published by Polystyle Publications and Century 21 Merchandising Ltd: 'Through the avenues and alley ways ...'.

in the *Alien* franchise, unwittingly disturb a bunch of hatchling aliens, the eggs having been laid in the stricken craft they had come to rescue.

Much of the impact of *Alien* was the deft way in which director Ridley Scott teased the audience, allowing them only brief glimpses of the terrifying and virtually indestructible monster, created from the fertile imagination of the European artist, H.R. Giger. To avoid weakening the impact of the film by publishing images of the Alien itself, or allowing toy or model replicas to be available before the movie had been widely seen, very little merchandise was available for the first film.

With the sequel, *Aliens* (1986), a kind of 'Vietnam war in space' action movie directed by James Cameron, much more was seen of the alien creatures and of the hardware used. Consequently, replicas of the *Nostro-*

mo, the Alien itself, the hydraulic heavy lifting gear that Sigourney Weaver uses as a weapon equivalent to the Alien's strength, and lots of other bits and pieces from the film were licensed and available to eager fans.

Kit manufacturer Halcyon led the way as far as *Aliens* construction kits were concerned, producing accurate scaled replicas of the *Nostromo* itself, an Alien 'face-hugger', Ripley's Class II Power Loader, the Sulaco Drop Ship and an Armoured Personnel Carrier.

I was fortunate enough to be involved with the marketing of *Aliens*, albeit for a very brief time. Whilst on the set, mostly located in a disused power station in Acton, west London, I noticed that the aforementioned APC was actually a conversion of one of the vehicles used on modern aircraft carriers. Designed to be low enough to pass under the wings of jet aircraft, the machines are very unusual out of context – ideal for converting into futuristic vehicles.

Of the wide range of figures of the reptilian Alien with the long and smooth-topped skull and the equally long but far sharper teeth with extending jaw, probably the best and most rare is Kenner's huge 18in (457mm) tall version. However, this toy, thought by most kids to be the height of cool, was withdrawn by Kenner after a wave of negative press reports and parental comments about the creepy beast with the glowing head keeping their children awake at night. Consequently this is a very rare 'toy'.

A quick scan of the internet confirms that all of the items produced under licence to *Aliens* and its successors ('vintage', not the many newer action figures and so on that are currently available) command premium prices amongst collectors. I only wish I had bought all the Halcyon kits when they were first available....

The *Alien* series was about one kind of invasion but dealt principally with the life-or-death struggle between unmatched opponents. With the Soviet invasion of Afghanistan in 1979, the decade ended with another battle between rivals with vastly differing capabilities. However, much like the movie, this ill-conceived operation proved how hard it was to overcome stubborn human resistance.

The launch of *Ariane*, the European Space Agency's challenge to NASA's space shuttle, only served to confirm that the 1980s began with a blast.

THE 1980s: TOP TV, THE BIG MOVIES, MEDIA EVENTS

Military Influence in the Early 1980s

In Britain, the early 1980s were defined by military action. On 30 April 1980 Iranian terrorists demanding a homeland for Khuzestan took over the Iranian embassy at Prince's Gate near Hyde Park in London. On 5 May 1980, the dramatic SAS operation to free the hostages was watched live on TV by a suppertime audience that marvelled at the equipment and tactics of the British Special Forces.

Until this moment, the Special Air Service was really only known for its World War Two hit-and-run raids in the western desert against Rommel's Afrika Korps. Now, everyone wanted to know more – books about the famous regiment's history and the story of its founder David Stirling sold by the thousand.

ABOVE: **On 5 May 1980, the dramatic SAS operation to free the hostages in the Iranian embassy was watched live on TV by the suppertime audience in Britain. The moment this top-secret army unit entered the limelight, everyone wanted to know more about them, as this 1980 publication shows.**

LEFT: **In 1983, British manufacturer Airfix released a set of fourteen highly detailed and very accurate 1/32 scale soft plastic SAS soldiers.**

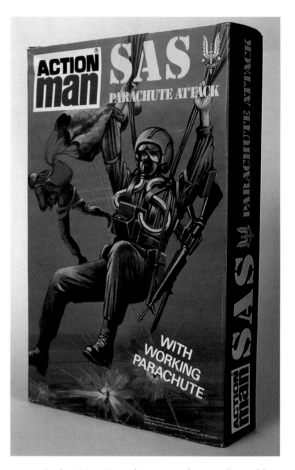

ABOVE: **Action Man 'Parachute Attack' set released in 1983. It featured a working parachute and a range of specialized accessories to use with existing SAS figures.**

'Action Man Special Operations SAS Commander' figure from 1983: 'Go into action with the legendary SAS. They dare. They win!'

With their own toy soldiers, young boys naturally wanted to mimic the operations they had seen on TV. It wasn't long before toy manufacturers met the demand for soldiers that looked the same as the black-clad troopers they had watched swinging through the embassy windows, lobbing stun grenades and brandishing distinctly non-service-issue machine pistols. Airfix was one of the manufacturers that satisfied this demand, releasing a pretty accurate set of 1/32 scale SAS troopers, appropriately clad in black, later in 1980.

The newfound-celebrity awarded to the SAS was also a blessing for Palitoy's Action Man. The famous 12in (305mm) fighting man had been fighting and losing a rearguard action with *Star Wars'* popular 3in (76mm) figures since 1977. In an effort to challenge this, Palitoy had introduced a new 'dynamic physique' to the toys which, together with the 'eagle eye' and 'gripping hands' features pioneered some years earlier, was intended to revitalize Action Man's appeal. Indeed, as a direct response to the science fantasy appeal of *Star Wars* characters like Han Solo and bounty hunter Boba Fett, Palitoy added a sci-fi element to the Action Man range with the introduction of 'Space Rangers' and 'Space Pirates'. However, it was the introduction of SAS characters within Action Man's ranks that most reflected the toy's traditional, manly appeal.

In the early 1980s the Action Man range was joined by an SAS Key Figure. Resplendent in black combat suit, grey hood, gas mask and armed with a miniature Heckler & Koch MP5 sub-machine gun, Browning pistol, grenades and even a grappling hook; for a while, this figure injected life into a tired product line.

An Action Man SAS Commander soon joined the range, but the icing on the cake was the trio of accessory sets that accompanied it. The SAS Parachute Attack set came complete with a working parachute; Secret Mission included a dinghy, parachute 'drop pod' weapons container, sticks of dynamite and a replica of the SA 80 – the British army's new rifle. The SAS Underwater Attack set revitalized an old favourite – Action Man's scuba gear. The sets all had brand new pieces, however, such as flak jackets, chest webbing arrangements and ammo vests. All of these new items also included black on yellow patches sporting the SAS's famous winged dagger.

Despite Palitoy introducing a range of 3in figures under the 'Action Force' banner, in direct competition with the *Star Wars* figures, and even though some of them were in SAS garb, the days of the traditional 12in Action Man doll were numbered. Production of Action Man ceased in 1984. Hasbro relaunched the famous brand in 1993, but with the focus on more politically correct adventure and espionage themes.

In 1982, the Falklands War would once more demonstrate Britain's military capabilities, giving another boost to manufacturers of what since the 1970s had increasingly become very unfashionable 'war toys'. And not since wartime days had modellers been able to make models of the ships, aircraft and vehicles actually involved in an overseas war.

Starring Jan-Michael Vincent, *Airwolf* was on our screens from 1984–86. This ERTL die-cast *Airwolf* helicopter dates from 1984 when the series was first transmitted.

Argentina was Britain's ally until it seized the Falkland Islands. Its armed forces were equipped with weapon systems very similar to those used by the British, French and Americans. Therefore, it was very easy for toy companies and kit manufacturers to adapt existing examples of French or American war machines

ABOVE: **In 1984, American kit manufacturer Monogram produced this 1/32 scale kit of the Blue Thunder helicopter.**

LEFT: **Directed by Ted Kotcheff and premiering in 1982, Sylvester Stallone played Vietnam veteran John J. Rambo in** *First Blood*. **US kit manufacturer Monogram combined two of their older models and repackaged them as a 'Rambo Attack Set' in association with the movie.**

simply by producing a new set of decals in Argentinean national colours – converting them to Exocet-firing Mirages, for example.

Nearing the end of their service life, parts of Britain's hastily assembled task force were well known. One vessel, HMS *Fearless*, an amphibious landing platform of the Royal Navy, had been launched in 1963. As long ago as 1968 a 1/600 scale kit of the assault ship had graced the pages of Airfix catalogues.

Plastic kits, Action Man SAS figures and even films and TV programmes were caught up in the wave of patriotism sweeping Britain at the beginning of the 1980s. The prowess of Britain's military and especially its Special Forces was a tonic to a nation, which had that year seen its international status diminish.

The 1982 British film *Who Dares Wins* starred Lewis Collins as Capt Peter Skellen of the SAS. After being dismissed from the regiment for excessive bullying and in search of a job that will use all his skills, Skellen joins the terrorist 'People's Lobby' and attempts to infiltrate their ranks and foil an attempt to kidnap American VIPs. Though panned by the critics for its corny script and dismissed by military enthusiasts (and no doubt the SAS as well) for its many inaccuracies, the film did well at the box office.

Lewis Collins fitted into the role of an SAS officer well. The actor had the persona of someone who could look after himself. In fact, since 1977 he had portrayed William Bodie, co-starring with Martin Shaw (Ray Doyle) and Gordon Jackson (CI5 boss George Cowley) in the hit TV series *The Professionals*. The show continued in production until 1983, straddling the period of the Prince's Gate siege and the Falklands War.

By the 1980s America had at last come to terms with the loss and waste of the Vietnam War. Movies like *The Deer Hunter* and *Platoon* showed US audiences the brutality and horrific futility of the war. Dealing with some of the real issues and the legacy of what was in fact a defeat was a cathartic act. One of the best TV shows to deal with the period was *Nam: Tour of Duty*, first broadcast in 1987. US kit manufacturer Monogram repackaged some of its kits, like this 1/48 scale Skyraider, and presented them in association with the series.

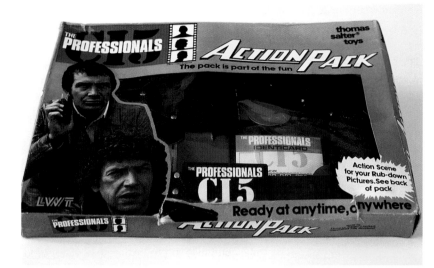

From 1977 until 1983, *The Professionals* – William Bodie, Ray Doyle and their CI5 boss George Cowley – held centre stage in the action/adventure field on British TV. This Thomas Salter Toys 'CI5 Action Pack' dates from 1978.

BELOW: *The Empire Strikes Back Annual* 1980.

There had been an appetite in Britain for stories about shadowy, but benign, covert security squads for a long time, partially because many perhaps felt insecure in a nation exposed to frequent terrorist outrages. In the 1970s, *The Sweeney* reassured TV audiences with the notion that the police had its own 'special force' – the Flying Squad – capable of taking care of things in the national interest. With its fictitious Whitehall intelligence department, CI5, *The Professionals* filled the vacuum left by *The Sweeney* and both programmes were the subject of annuals, toys and games.

Star Wars Parts V and VI

On the other side of the Atlantic, the 1980s kicked off with the next instalment in the *Star Wars* saga. Although *The Empire Strikes Back* was Lucas's second film in the series, it was actually episode V in the saga. In outline, the story dealt with Luke Skywalker's efforts to master the ways of the Jedi knights, spending a lot of time learning from Yoda, the wise, small and green Jedi Master. Meanwhile, Darth Vader and his cohorts continued in their attempt to quash the rebellion and capture Luke in the process.

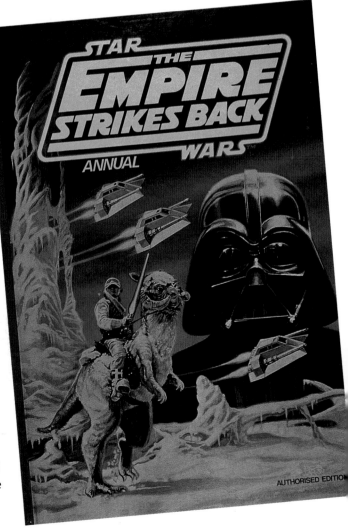

Though there were lots of clashing light sabres and explosions, as with all the Lucas-penned *Star Wars* scripts, *The Empire Strikes Back* also showed humanity in its most honourable light. The film was a massive success and a great tonic in a world often full of the same old human failings of expansionist war and politically motivated terrorism.

The success of the 1977 film had taken many by surprise. As a result, 20th Century Fox and those lucky enough to have toy and licensed concessions weren't going to be caught out in 1980. By then, the *Star Wars* merchandising juggernaut with which we are all familiar today was well under way.

US toy giant Kenner merely had to rebrand its earlier *Star Wars* 3in figures, releasing the old *Star Wars* 'twenty-one backs' in new *The Empire Strikes Back* branding. Curiously, though, some of these are rarer than certain *Star Wars* figures released three years previously.

MPC and Airfix, which possessed the plastic construction kit concession respectively in the USA and Great Britain, produced a range of stunning replicas based on the movie. Their large-scale individual AT-AT (All Terrain Armoured Transport) replica was excellently produced. However, a sister construction kit from the same manufacturer, 'Battle on Ice Planet Hoth', also featuring the lumbering AT-ATs, eclipsed even this.

The Snap-Fix set came complete with a vac-formed, pre-printed one-piece diorama base and featured miniature gun batteries and even a couple of tiny snowspeeders. Simply by the addition of lengths of fuse wire, modellers could recreate the scene where the snowspeeders attempt to lasso the dinosaur-like monsters, causing the AT-ATs to stumble and crash to the ground.

Airfix wasn't finished there, however, as it also produced a highly detailed replica of bounty hunter Boba Fett's spaceship. To me, this vehicle looked like a giant mutated flying flat iron.

All of the British (Airfix) models and the MPC (US) originals relating to *The Empire Strikes Back* are extremely collectable, with mint and boxed versions naturally more so. Collectors should note, however, that at the

Like all of the other *Star Wars* kits produced by Airfix, this AT-AT was manufactured using tools developed in the United States for Airfix by subsidiaries of General Mills – the huge US conglomerate which, a year later, would save the firm from receivership.

Super and highly collectable licence-built Airfix kit of Luke Skywalker's snowspeeder from *The Empire Strikes Back*.

RIGHT: **1980 vintage Airfix kit of bounty hunter Boba Fett's spaceship, Slave I, as featured in the *Star Wars* movie, *The Empire Strikes Back*.**

time they were released, Airfix seemed to be experimenting with much thinner, and presumably cheaper, packaging carton for its boxes. The Airfix kit of Boba Fett's ship, *Slave I*, was certainly packaged in a very flimsy box. The addition of shrink-wrapping, which Airfix had recently introduced to seal kit boxes and prevent canny modellers from spuriously requesting 'missing' spare parts, tended to deform the box rather than protect it.

Although the various kits of the AT-AT were popular, the version every young boy wanted was the toy one manufactured in 1981 by Palitoy. This highly detailed and fully articulated version was simply huge. The cockpit in the machine's 'head' could accommodate two 3in figures to drive it. Clad in white body armour, a further ten stormtroopers fitted within the beast's hull. Such was their popularity, *Star Wars* toys were voted 'Toy of the Year 1982' by the British Toy Retailers Association.

Star Wars fans didn't have long to wait for the next instalment in the unfolding story of Luke, Han and Princess Leia: *Return of the Jedi* (episode VI) premiered in 1983. This time, the story, really the conclusion of the entire epic even though there would be three 'prequels' twenty years later, focused on Han Solo's escape from the palace of Jabba the Hutt and on Luke's attempts, after his discovery that his father was actually the evil Darth Vader, to bring his bad dad back to the good side of 'the Force'.

Manufacturers fortunate enough to be holding the golden ticket of a *Star Wars* toy concession enjoyed the usual bounteous payouts. Children flocked to purchase toys featuring Jabba (a Palitoy diorama showing the slug-like creature smoking a hookah pipe with his pet, the fawning Salacious Crumb, on a leash nearby, proved enormously popular), Ewoks, speeder bikes and Tauntauns. The very luckiest children received toy replicas of the Death Star, which was after all the main focus of the film. Death Stars were available in a variety

American manufacturer Kenner had secured the toy concession for the 1983 film *Return of the Jedi*. After being caught on the back foot by the enormous success of *Star Wars* in 1977, by the 1980s manufacturers were well prepared. This mint and boxed speeder bike sold by the ton. Despite featuring a photograph of a stormtrooper astride the vehicle and a spear-carrying Ewok by its side, figures were sold separately.

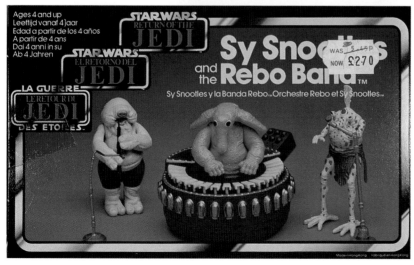

LEFT: Normally I remove stickers and bits of tape from toy packaging, cleaning the boxes up before I photograph them, but I couldn't resist leaving the price tag on this Kenner toy of Sy Snootles and the Rebo Band. After the initial excitement about the 1983 release *Return of the Jedi* had died down, British store Boots reduced the original price of £5.45 to a measly £2.70 to ensure a sale in 1984. Today, this very collectable vignette, mint and boxed, would sell for at least fifteen times the original asking price!

of sizes, some converted into carrying cases designed to hold a growing collection of 3in figures. In 1983 *Star Wars* carried off 'Toy of the Year' for a second time.

ABOVE: **US manufacturer Kenner supported the 1983 release of *Return of the Jedi* with a huge range of their ever-popular 3in action figures. Keen-eyed collectors will gasp at how little British retailer Tesco asked for this figure of Boba Fett at the time of the film's release. This figure is allegedly the most valuable of those released at the time and is worth up to £1,000 in such a mint, 'carded' state**

ABOVE RIGHT: **Although there is an enormous selection of figures to collect, perhaps two of the most iconic are of the 'droids' C-3PO and R2-D2. The figures shown here feature details such as Artoo's 'Sensorscope' attachment and Threepio's removable limbs, which add to their value.**

RIGHT: ***Return of the Jedi Annual* 1983.**

US manufacturer LJN
produced a range of toys
licensed from the film
interpretation of Frank
Herbert's classic novels. This
Dune Sandworm toy was a
'large poseable monster from
beneath the desert surface'.

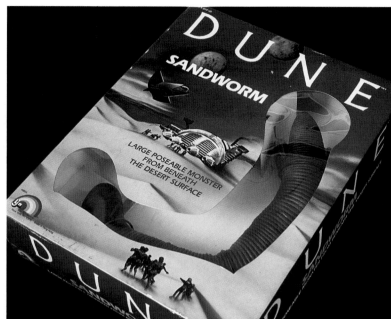

BELOW: In 1984 Parker Brothers
produced this lavish board
game in association with
the release of the sci-fi
movie *Dune*.

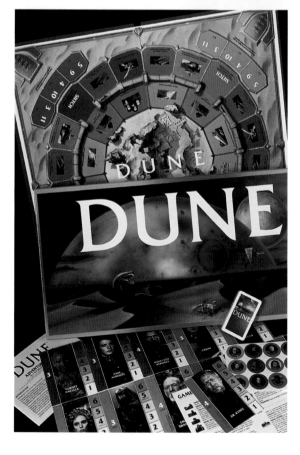

ABOVE: The TV series *Star Trek: The Next Generation*
was produced between 1987 and 1994. A carded 3in
Romulan figure from Japanese manufacturer Bandai
is shown. Thousands of these figures survive loose;
finding pristine carded examples should be the goal
of the collector.

A pair of Waddington's jigsaw puzzles based on the 1982 film *Tron*.

BELOW: Shish Kebab Beetlejuice action figure (with scary skewers), manufactured by Kenner in 1998.

RIGHT: Carded ERTL die-cast miniature of a Klingon Bird of Prey from the 1989 movie, *Star Trek V – The Final Frontier*.

Spielberg Dominates the 1980s

By the mid-1970s, not withstanding the trail-blazing movies *Westworld* (1973), *Rollerball* (1975) and *Logan's Run* (1976), the success of the original *Star Wars* film had demonstrated audiences' appetites for science fiction. The two early-eighties Lucas Film blockbusters continued to encourage producers to look for stories set in the techno-logically advanced future. However, one movie in the same genre was set in the suburban American present. *E.T. the Extra-Terrestrial* was Steven Spielberg's 1982 foray in the sci-fi genre, but without the need to resort to laser beams, explosions and duelling spaceships.

The film tells the story of a young boy, Elliott, who discovers a cute alien. He keeps him secretly at home, for fear of attracting unwanted media or governmental attention, then helps the wayward space traveller find his way home.

E.T. was the movie's star and a vast assortment of figures of him – both large and small, in either rigid plastic or soft plush – were manufactured. Most of these featured E.T.'s outstretched hand and glowing fingertip. With his catchphrase, 'E.T. phone home', the alien was a natural for the promotion of phones, his image being used by many telecommunication companies as well as some phones being manufactured in his likeness.

Some of the most popular items were moneyboxes, as the extraterrestrial's large head and squat body lent themselves ideally to such a purpose. There were also 8in (203mm) picture discs of the movie's theme with a picture of E.T. on one side and the famous moonlit bike ride on the reverse.

'Calling Avon' ladies included a limited edition cosmetic in their 1982 offering. The special limited-edition E.T. soap came in a box featuring images from the

LJN bendable Stripe figure – one of the creatures from the 1984 movie, *Gremlins*.

film; the soap block also had similar images printed onto it, but also featured the legend 'E.T. & Elliott Together Again'.

The year before *E.T.*, the prolific Steven Spielberg's *Raiders of the Lost Ark* was released. This, the first in the series of movies starring Harrison Ford as the archaeologist cum adventurer Indiana Jones, was more along the traditional lines of adventure stories that radio audiences in the 1930s might have enjoyed. It was non-stop thrills and spills from start to finish.

Surprisingly for such a successful film, very few toys were licensed from it and the following sequels. Annuals and graphic novels were produced of course, but in my opinion the crème de la crème has to be Kenner's 12in 'large-size action figure' of 'Indy' released in 1981 when the film was first screened. This figure, dressed in Indy's signature brown trousers, leather jacket and cowboy hat, was the same size as the larger *Star Wars* figures that Kenner produced. It also came with his trademark bullwhip and Kenner's TV commercial showed the doll using it to good purpose lassoing nearby branches in order to lift the hero away from danger.

Released in 1984, Joe Dante's film *Gremlins* was another sci-fi movie in a similar mould to *E.T.* However, whereas the extraterrestrial in the former movie was cute, the Gremlins, as everyone knows, looked cute but weren't. The wide-eyed creatures seen on film were the ideal progenitors for toys and a range of vinyl and plush Gremlins in a variety of sizes rapidly became available.

A miniature wind-up E.T. toy from 1982 manufactured by LJN and another *Gremlins* toy, Stripe and Gizmo's Storage Pot, from the same manufacturer.

Enter the Cyborgs

The Terminator, starring Arnold Schwarzenegger in the days before he was Governor of California, was released in 1984. The story of a virtually indestructible cyborg sent back in time to kill the mother of the leader of a future rebellion, the movie was a huge success and to date has spawned two sequels.

The Terminator itself is seen in varying states of physical integrity at different points in the movie. Sometimes it is clad in a leather biker jacket and jeans; at other times it is seen with its outer 'skin' torn and elements of its internal circuitry and mechanics showing. Finally, after emerging from the conflagration of a burning petrol tanker, the Terminator's metal endoskeleton is revealed and the machine is reduced to its bare frame.

A blockbuster movie featuring a robotic star in several differing guises was a real boon to toy and model manufacturers, who quickly discovered they could maximize their returns on tooling by offering several versions from the same basic moulds. Kenner and other manufacturers produced the now almost obligatory 3in and 6in (152mm) action figures, whilst model companies, most noticeably the plethora of small 'garage firms', went to work producing a range of Terminator replicas using resin kit components.

Resin construction kits were an innovation of the 1980s. A far cheaper production method than polystyrene injection moulding, they provided an accessible entry level into the construction kit market for small operators. Although the flexible moulds used to cast resin kits were capable of resolving fine detail, they were not as durable as the machine-steel tools traditionally used by Airfix, Revell, Monogram and the like. Consequently, resin kits were often produced in very short runs – which only adds to their collectability. Some of the best came from Japan.

Paul Verhoeven's 1987 film, *RoboCop*, was set in Detroit in the near future. A terminally wounded policeman is rebuilt by OCP, a corporate giant which has the franchise for policing in the city. The resulting half-man, half-machine cybernetic cop is called Robo-Cop. Though he is seemingly a hard-wired and impersonal law-enforcement robot, his memory banks retain just enough of the character and integrity of Murphy, the late officer.

Like the Terminator, RoboCop himself was a natural subject for kit manufacturers to turn into construction kits. And again, as with the Schwarzenegger movie, most of these models were in short-run resin form.

The RoboCop wasn't the only mechanical star in the show. In an effort to get rid of RoboCop, who had

AMT/ERTL's kit of Officer Murphy's Robo 1 police car, as featured in the hit 1987 movie *RoboCop*. This release was available when the sequel, *RoboCop 2*, was produced.

BELOW LEFT: **Extremely desirable 'Billiken' tin-plate RoboCop figure from the 1980s.**

BELOW RIGHT: **Two differing versions of Corgi's 1/36 scale die-cast No. 272 Citroën 2CV from the 1981 James Bond movie, *For Your Eyes Only*, starring Roger Moore.**

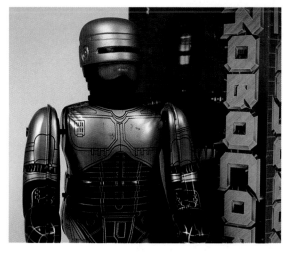

discovered that OCP was complicit in drug running and other organized crimes in Detroit, a heavily armed, but thankfully totally inept, droid classified as ED-209 was turned on him. Many of the Japanese kit manufacturers in particular produced models of RoboCop and the chunkier ED-209, enabling those used to working in the larger scales (1/8 or 1/10) to create some stunning dioramas.

Perhaps one of the most attractive, and certainly today one of the most collectable, items is Billiken's love-ly tin-plate clockwork RoboCop. Beautifully litho-printed, a couple of turns of the key enables the man-machine to walk along with his arms moving up and down.

US giant Kenner produced a range of 3in figures under licence to the film's producers. They were super-detailed – RoboCop even had a removable helmet and separate pistol (this impressive weapon was also produced in a range of toy BB guns).

Other Film and TV Spin-Offs of the 1980s

Plastic construction kits were ideal spin-offs related to *Back to the Future*, the time-travelling film starring Michael J. Fox, which hit the screens in 1985. This was not very surprising, I suppose – the film's time machine was a converted DeLorean. Model car manufacturer AMT and Japanese kit firm Aoshima produced some particularly good kits.

Top Gun, the Tom Cruise movie about crack US Navy fighter pilots, brought cinema audiences back to contemporary reality when it was released in 1986. No aliens, time travellers or cyborgs here, just a decent script, well-defined characters and some stunning air-to-air cinematography of jet fighter planes. Many of the aircraft featured in the film had been in service for years, while some were relatively new, but all of them appeared in a variety of manufacturers' kit catalogues.

Airfix was granted the British licence to produce associated kits. In the throes of being sold by Palitoy to Humbrol, Airfix hastily repackaged a trio of existing

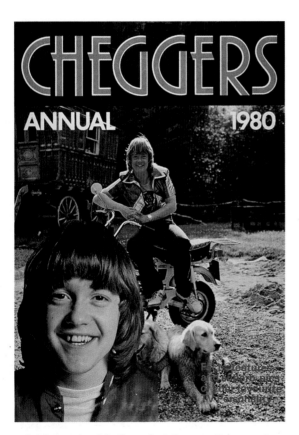

A fresh-faced Keith Chegwin ('Cheggers') graces the cover of his own annual in 1980.

With his weekly *Video Show*, the late Kenny Everett brought the wacky and irreverent persona he had developed on London's Capital Radio to Thames TV. This annual dates from 1980.

LEFT: Directed by ex-Monkee Micky Dolenz, *Metal Mickey* was on British TV between 1980–83. However, the robotic character often popped up on other programmes and his popularity continued long after his series had been canned, as this annual from 1985 confirms.

BELOW LEFT: Good old Dusty Bin: *3–2–1 Annual* from 1985.

ABOVE: Electronic 'Name That Tune' game from Tom O'Connor's popular TV game show. Complete with song book, prize money and instrument, this toy was manufactured in 1979 by Peter Pan Playthings.

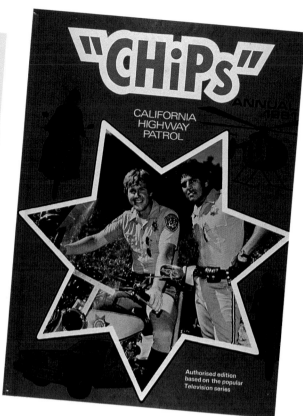

ABOVE LEFT: ERTL 1/64 scale die-cast of David Hasselhoff's talking car, KITT (Knight Industries Two Thousand) from TV's *Knight Rider*. This toy was manufactured in 1982; the series was produced between 1982–86.

ABOVE: The *CHiPs* (California Highway Patrol) TV series was produced for six years between 1977–83. This annual dates from 1981.

LEFT: 'Michael Jackson Authentic Stage Outfit': With glittering 'magic' glove, 'Will fit most 12in dolls', proclaimed the text on this Grammy Awards Outfit manufactured by LJN in association with MJJ Productions in 1984.

1/72 kits and branded them 'As seen in *Top Gun*'. Consequently, the firm's F-5E Tiger II, F-14 Tomcat and venerable A-4 Skyhawk enjoyed a new lease of life in boxes with pictures of Tom Cruise and Kelly McGillis on the lids!

Predator, another Arnold Schwarzenegger sci-fi blockbuster, was released in 1987. Very soon, Kenner, which also produced a range of *Aliens* toys and had released a very popular and now very collectable '*Aliens* Queen

How cool was Fonzie? *Happy Days Annual* from 1981.

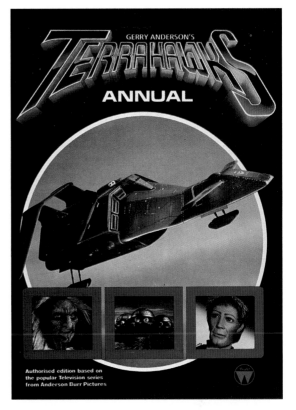

Gerry Anderson and Christopher Burr's *Terrahawks* was transmitted between 1983–84. This annual is from 1983.

Hive' playset, began coupling the Alien with the dreadlock-wearing Predator. Comic strips and a film series of the encounters between the two monsters were soon available. Vintage toys of the Alien versus the Predator are now very collectable among enthusiasts.

In 1989, although both *Indiana Jones and the Last Crusade* and Tim Burton's *Batman* received their fair share of attention from the usual publishers and toy and game manufacturers, the only two really quite different films of the late 1980s were *Rain Man* and *Who Framed Roger Rabbit?*, both released in 1988. Of these, naturally only the latter film, which was part live action and part animation, had toy-spin-off value. Consequently, a range of miniature cartoon characters, principally of the eponymous rabbit, was produced.

Not to be outdone, the stalwart Gerry Anderson and his team also released a new series in the 1980s.

Made between 1983–84, the thirty-nine twenty-four-minute episodes of *Terrahawks* was Anderson's return to his traditional world of puppets in space. Set in the year 2020, *Terrahawks* told the story of a group of heroes led by Tiger Ninestein who, equipped with a range of five main spacecraft, attempt to defeat the evil powers of the erstwhile android bodyguard, Zelda of the planet Guk.

The *Terrahawks* spacecraft (Terrahawk, Hawkwing, Battlehawk, Treehawk and Spacehawk) were typical of the classic designs that have always come from Anderson's studios and were very popular. However, as far as children were concerned, the real stars of the show were the Zeroids, designed by Ninestein's technology wizard, Lt Hiro.

There were three principal Zeroids, each built around an 'Iranium crystal power source' found only on Jupiter.

Japanese manufacturer Bandai produced an excellent range of toys licensed from *Terrahawks*. Together with the other toys in Bandai's extensive range, the carded Space Sergeant 101 and the boxed Terrahawk shown in the photograph are now becoming quite sought after amongst Anderson's myriad fans.

RIGHT: **Bandai produced a range of fifteen craft from *Terrahawks* and here's a loose Hawkwing. It is complete with all its missiles (one is loaded ready to be fired). As long as they are complete with all accessories, even loose such as here, are worth collecting.**

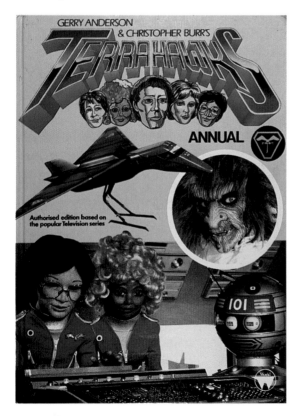

LEFT: **This is the second *Terrahawks Annual*, published in 1984.**

Quickly, Sgt Major Zero, Space Sgt 101 and the spherical Number 13 developed their own distinctive fanbase.

Japanese toy and model giant Bandai secured the rights to produce *Terrahawks* toys under licence to the short-lived series. The die-cast replicas of the various spacecraft and Zeroids were manufactured to very high standards. Beautifully packaged and presented, these toys are now becoming very collectable. Enthusiastic collectors should ensure that the most rare, the mint and boxed examples, still contain accessories such as the tiny orange missiles that came with and could actually be fired from the various *Terrahawk* spacecraft.

RIGHT: *The A-Team* was produced between 1983–87. These 1983 vintage carded Galoob fully poseable action figures of Hannibal and Mr. T are complete with a range of miniature accessories.

ABOVE: Bluebird manufactured this Big Badge featuring Mr T in 1984.

BELOW: American manufacturer Galoob didn't only produce 3in A-Team action figures. This super large-scale Mr. T doll from the mid 1980s is an example of their more ambitious productions. Mint and boxed and in superb condition, this replica of the 'real-life superhero' even came complete with real chains, medallion, earrings and bracelets!

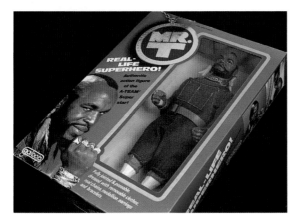

RIGHT: Some merchandised items, such as stationery sets, rarely survive complete and intact; however, this A-Team Writing Set has.

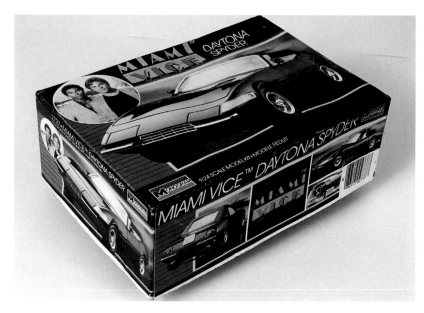

Miami Vice was produced between 1984–89. This Monogram 1/24 scale plastic construction kit of Tubbs' and Crocket's car, a Daytona Spyder, was produced in 1985.

BELOW: Hunky actor Tom Selleck played US detective Magnum in the hit series *Magnum P.I.* This Corgi die-cast pairing of a US police car with Magnum's own Ferrari 308 dates from 1980.

Of the remaining top TV shows of the 1980s, a range of annuals produced in association with hit shows like *Dallas*, *Dynasty*, *The Golden Girls* and *Roseanne*, for example, have since become quite scarce and collect-able. The other big shows – *The A-Team*, *The Dukes of Hazzard*, *Magnum P.I.*, *The Fall Guy* and *Miami Vice* each received the attention of the manufacturers of action figures and die-cast vehicles.

THE 1990s: TOP TV, THE BIG MOVIES, MEDIA EVENTS

In the 1990s, British TV supported the rise and rise of the reality make-over phenomenon. Gardeners had always enjoyed regular TV shows, usually presented by Alan Titchmarsh but now supplemented by the bra-less charms and equally obvious gardening skills of Charlie Dimmock. Celebrities in the making Diarmuid Gavin and the more robust Tommy Walsh added to the revitalization of a genre long associated with the more genteel approach of Percy Thrower.

A range of home DIY programmes joined these more traditional programmes, with the BBC's *Changing Rooms* in the vanguard. These showed viewers how to spice up their home décor with a lick of paint, some MDF and a variety of carefully located uplighters.

Airfix 2-kit Desert Storm gift set released in 1991. The box contained two 1/72 scale kits: a Buccaneer S.2B and a BAC Jaguar GR1.

The First Gulf War

Sadly, televisions in the early 1990s also showed the reality of the First Gulf War of 1990–91. At the time, the swift victory of the allied coalition was mostly met with a feeling of relief that on the Anglo-American side at least casualties were relatively low. However, we now know that the legacy of the first incomplete campaign would require another war and lead to the so-called 'war on terrorism' that we have inherited in the twenty-first century.

Manufacturers of boys' toys felt duty-bound to provide die-cast replicas of Abrams and Challenger tanks and kit manufacturers grouped together examples of many of the aircraft and vehicles used into Operation *Desert Shield* compendiums.

Of course, the single most startling technological development of the First Gulf War was the US military's application of stealth and smart technologies. Conse-

quently, die-casts and model kits of equipment ranging from Patriot or Scud missiles and their launchers to tiny representations of the apparently breath-taking American Cruise missiles were on many a young boy's wants list.

Of perhaps more interest – certainly to kit manufacturers – were the new stealth fighters and bombers that the US employed in combat for the first time in 1991. The F-117, which looked as if it had come straight from a George Lucas movie, was perhaps the most intriguing. This fighter led the early pinpoint raids on Baghdad in 1991. Soon afterwards, a variety of kit manufacturers produced replicas of this amazing aircraft, which proved invisible to Iraqi air defences. At the time, a popular joke amongst British modellers awaiting the new

F-117 from Airfix was that it would probably consist of a box containing a pilot and nothing more.

The First Gulf War seemed to many children to be a synthesis of computer games and all the exciting war films they'd seen. The reality of the war, as shown by the horrendous TV images of the Iraqi retreat from Kuwait on the aptly named 'Highway of Death', was all too macabre.

Hollywood Blockbusters of the 1990s

Fortunately, TV and cinema audiences clearly wanted a modicum of unreality too, which the success of the decade's first smash hit movie, Steven Spielberg's *Jurassic Park*, proved when it was released to packed houses in 1993. *Jurassic Park*, a tale of an eccentric billionaire who builds a theme park on a remote island full of dinosaurs cloned from DNA trapped in amber for millions of years, was a natural to exploit as far as toy merchandise was concerned. Not since Raquel Welch speared one of Ray Harryhausen's stop-motion Allosaurus's in *One Million Years BC* (1966) had dinosaurs been so popular.

US toy giant Kenner was the first to secure the concession from Amblin Entertainment to produce toys licensed from the first film in the series, originally producing five figures that were bubble- or blister-mounted on a card back. Also produced were a range of vehicles seen in the movie. Amongst them, the Jungle Explorer vehicle came with a Dino Damaged Hood and a cannon on the pick-up back capable of firing blood sample missiles. All pretty exciting stuff and scaled to accommodate the figures of Tim Murphy, who came complete with a retracting snare and a small dinosaur to lasso, and Robert Muldoon, who came with the obligatory dinosaur, this time an aggressive Raptor, hence his armament consisting of a tranquillizer-firing bazooka!

Other early vehicles included a Bush Devil Tracker jeep that was heavily armed. This vehicle had the tranq-missile firing launcher together with a boom-mounted dinosaur snare. For added realism, it also featured battle damage inflicted by angry dinosaurs.

One of the coolest machines was the Jurassic Park capture 'copter. It fired tranquillizing missiles from an under-slung launcher, but was also equipped with a net capable of ensnaring escaped dinosaurs and a winch so that the beasts could be transported back into captivity.

All *Jurassic Park* action figures, vehicles and other associated models, toys and games are worth holding

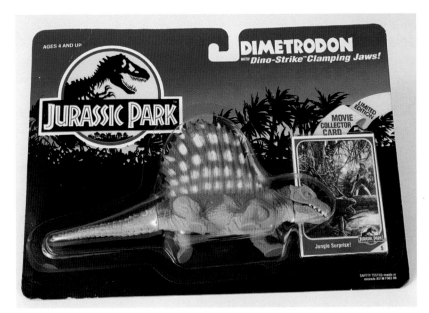

**Kenner Jurassic Park
Dimetrodon with 'Dino-Strike
Clamping Jaws' and limited-
edition movie card from 1993.**

Super and very collectable Halcyon 1/2400 scale USS *Sulaco* from the 1992 blockbuster, *Alien 3*.

on to, but obviously those produced for the first movie are the most valuable. However, it is now nearly ten years since the sequel, *The Lost World: Jurassic Park*, was released and the merchandise for this is becoming rarer. Naturally, with time, those produced in association with the third movie based on Michael Crichton's novel, which was premiered as recently as 2001, will also appreciate in value.

Despite MTV's *Beavis and Butt-Head* attracting the attentions of older kids and in turn that of manufacturers keen to exploit a market, it was Hollywood that was really capable of driving demand. Released in 1994, *Stargate* continued with the ever-popular science fiction and fantasy theme.

It should be noted that despite their box-office appeal, one reason films such as *RoboCop*, *The Terminator*, *Star Wars* and *Jurassic Park* are eminently suitable for the production of toy spin-offs is that they largely feature purely fictitious characters, machines and equipment created by the imaginations of writers and designers. Consequently, manufacturers are not forced to get trademark agreements and so on from third parties that own the rights to existing vehicles and equipment currently used in 'reality'. For example, unless an Ancient Egyptian pharaoh was actually reincarnated (and had twentieth-century legal representation), the producers

and licence holders that manufactured toys associated with 1994's *Stargate* were free to do what they wanted. Actually, with Dean Devlin's script, the designers of Roland Emmerich's movie had some of the most original weapons and warriors to create and Kurt Russell and James Spader some of the most awesome foes to fight.

America's Hasbro produced a range of exciting toys co-ordinated for release with the movie. These included a range of 3in (76mm) action figures that naturally included representations of the movie's human stars, such as Kurt Russell, but also included replicas of the fantastic Ancient Egyptians, in a parallel universe on the other side of the Stargate. Two of my favourite figures are the chief guard, Anubis, who came blister-packed and complete with a fantastic head piece and accessories that included 'a collectable winged glider artefact', and Horus, who sported an even more fantastic headdress in the shape of a golden eagle and was packaged with a 'collectable chariot artefact'.

The other big movies of 1994 were *The Lion King* and *Forrest Gump*, although science fiction was as popular as ever. *Independence Day*, released in 1996, and *Men in Black*, which premiered the following year, both starred Will Smith – one of the most successful actors of the 1990s and beyond – and each attracted the attention of the toy business.

With its spaceships and aliens, *Independence Day* had more opportunities for exploitation, certainly amongst older children, than did *The Lion King*, which was subject to the more traditional pre-school plush toys, cereal premiums and book/video merchandise

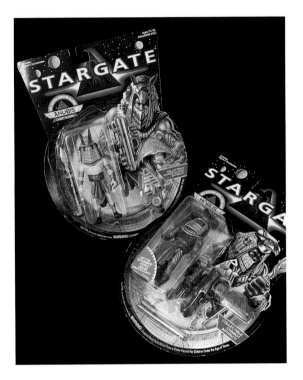

development. The licence for kit production related to *Independence Day* was secured by US plastic kit veteran, Lindberg. Rival US manufacturers Revell, Monogram and Aurora generally secured the lucrative movie concessions, so it was surprising that Lindberg won the licence for *ID4*, as it was generally known. Lindberg's kits, especially its replica of a Captured Alien Attacker, were of a remarkably high quality. The Attacker, for example, came complete with a stand that was accurate in every detail to the three-pronged restraint used by the human scientific team trying to discover a weakness in the machine's fabric or handling qualities, which the pilots of the US Air Force and its allies could then exploit to thwart the extraterrestrial domination of Earth

In 1997, *Titanic* and *The Lost World: Jurassic Park* were the most successful movies. The following year it was the turn of *Armageddon*, the story of a huge asteroid on course to decimate Earth, stopped by deep-core drilling team-cum-astronauts led by Bruce Willis.

No new movie, however epic, could hope to compete with the excitement and hype generated by the return of George Lucas's *Star Wars* series.

Released in May 1999, *Star Wars Episode I – The Phantom Menace*, was the first new *Star Wars* movie since *Return of the Jedi* – a gap of sixteen years. Lucas's new movie was eagerly awaited and the gap meant it would also appeal to a new generation of toy buyers.

ABOVE: **Two Hasbro 6in action figures from the 1994 movie *Stargate*. An Anubis Chief Guard and a Horus Attack Pilot.**

Monogram 1/20 scale construction kit of a Stinger from the US TV series *SeaQuest DSV*, which was only broadcast between 1993–96. Kits associated with short-run series like SeaQuest were obviously produced in relatively limited numbers and are consequently very collectable.

Fortunately, *Star Wars'* devotees are so loyal, the new film's producers were confident that veteran fans who purchased much of the associated merchandising in the 1970s and 1980s, would also snap up items related to the new film.

Following, the story of the young Anakin Skywalker (Darth Vader) and his relationship with Jedi Knights

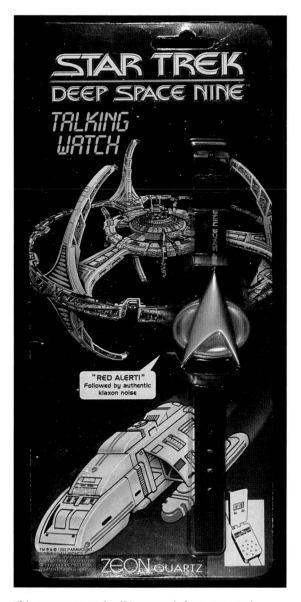

This quartz crystal talking watch from *Star Trek: Deep Space Nine* was manufactured in 1993. The series was produced between 1993 and 1999.

Obi-Wan Kenobi and Qui-Gon Jinn as they attempt to help Queen Amidala save her world from greedy trade executives (as well as the 'humorous' Jar Jar Binks and evil of evils, Darth Maul), *The Phantom Menace* was chock-a-block with new characters and vehicles.

Such was the anticipation for the new movie and its related merchandise that when product was available in the shops there was near pandemonium. On 18 June 1999, British newspaper *The Guardian* published a piece by journalist Libby Brooks entitled '*Phantom Menace* Merchandise Puts Toy Shops on Alert'. 'Toy shops across the country opened at midnight, predicting massive demand as merchandising from the film goes on sale in the UK today,' she began. 'In what has been heralded as the biggest merchandising campaign in cinema history, all sixty-one Toys 'R' Us stores have created special *Star Wars* zones, guarded by characters from the film and protected by a 7ft long Naboo Star Fighter overhead, while Hamley's toy store in central London has opened a Destination *Star Wars* shop within the store.'

Naturally, *Phantom Menace* toys sold like hot cakes. The new wave of 3in figures now came complete with sound chips (Commtech chips), which, if slotted into the optional reader, played sound bites from the movie. Technology had progressed sufficiently during the previous sixteen years and memory chips had dropped in price enough to allow the new toys – action figures of the floppy-eared Jar Jar Binks, light-sabre-wielding Darth Maul, robotic Battle Droids or vehicles, most notably the imaginative Pod Racers – to possess many more electronic features.

The James Bond franchise continued as well. Timothy Dalton played agent 007 in only two films: *The Living Daylights* in 1987 and 1989's *Licence to Kill* – the first Bond movie not based on an original Ian Fleming story. Both these movies were very successful and were responsible for toy spin-offs, which included a Corgi Aston Martin Volante from *The Living Daylights* and a Matchbox boxed set from *A Licence To Kill*, which included miniature replicas of the articulated fuel transporter, light aircraft, helicopter and pick-up truck as seen in the movie.

After a silence of six years – a long time in the world of Bond films – his licence to kill was restored when

Pierce Brosnan assumed the role of Bond. Brosnan made three 007 films in the 1990s, *Golden Eye* in 1995, *Tomorrow Never Dies* in 1997 and *The World is Not Enough* in 1999.

Corgi was one of the manufacturers to secure the British die-cast toy vehicle concessions for the Bond

LEFT: **This Japanese 1/6 scale Tsukuda short-run resin kit of the Terminator's Cyberdyne 800 Series endoskeleton is from the 1990 movie, *Terminator 2*.**

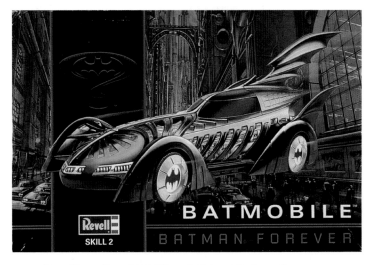

ABOVE: **Revell's replica of Val Kilmer's Batmobile from the 1995 movie, *Batman Forever*.**

RIGHT: **In 1997, actor George Clooney played the caped crusader in *Batman & Robin*. Actress Alicia Silverstone played Batgirl in the movie and this is a limited edition Kenner figure of her in her starring role.**

movies. The company produced an excellent replica of James Bond's BMW Z3 car from *Goldeneye*. Controversially, this vehicle – a move away from Bond's traditional British Aston Martins – was launched in concert with the film's release. The joint promotion was backed by a massive BMW advertising campaign for its hot new car and was an object lesson in the way movie marketing had evolved since the days of simple 'product placement'.

For *Tomorrow Never Dies*, Corgi released a stunning replica of Bond's latest car, another BMW, this time a 750i. This super little 1/36 scale replica even featured a pop-up chain cutter.

For *The World is Not Enough*, Corgi produced another 1/36 scale replica. The car this time was a sleek BMW Z8 and featured accurate representations of BMW's spoked wheels, chromed wing mirrors, a fully fitted interior and a pair of working side-mounted missiles. After all it was 'a Bond car'!

Among a series of five, including retro figures linked to *Thunderball*, *Goldeneye*, *Tomorrow Never Dies* and *The Spy Who Loved Me*, a limited-edition Action Man figure was also produced in association with *The World is Not Enough*. None of these excellent items was cheap when first available, now, in only a few years, their values have risen dramatically.

Gerry Anderson Continues

Re-runs of *Thunderbirds* on TV were as popular as ever, with Thunderbirds Tracy Island becoming one of the most popular-ever British toys in 1992. So popular, in fact, that this toy by manufacturer Vivid Imaginations sold out and long queues of hopeful children and their parents formed outside toy shops. Because of these shortages, Tracy Island narrowly lost out in total sales to another TV-related toy that year as Hasbro's WWF Wrestlers scooped the prize.

Despite *Thunderbirds*' continued popularity, Gerry Anderson, as one would expect, had a new series for the 1990s – *Space Precinct*. This was broadcast over twenty-four episodes on BBC 2 and on Sky TV between 1994–95. It was set in the year 2040 and told the story of former NYPD detective, Patrick Brogan. Now a Lieutenant with the Demeter City police force on the planet Altor, Brogan and his colleagues investigate crimes committed by the usual human suspects but by weird aliens too.

Vivid Imaginations produced a range of toys licensed to *Space Precinct*. Amongst them, the 'twelve-back' 3in figure sets included miniature replicas of Lt Brogan, Captain Podly, aliens Morgo, Officer Took and the robot, Slomo, each blister packed complete with accessories

1960s British TV series *Thunderbirds* is eternally popular. Produced in the 1990s, this Japanese kit from manufacturer Imai features the classic Thunderbird 2 in its container dock and is complete with a selection of the craft's pods and their alternative contents.

Space Precinct annual 1994.

BELOW: Because of its relatively short life, toys licensed to *Space Precinct* are increasingly hard to find in any condition – mint ones in their original packaging even more so. The Space Precinct Police Bike and Lieutenant Brogan figure shown here were manufactured by Vivid Imaginations in 1994.

In the early 1990s manufacturer Vivid Imaginations produced this lovely, and quite substantial, Stingray toy. It worked in water and with a few winds the super sub's engine could be made to revolve, propelling the craft forwards.

This version of my favourite Gerry Anderson creation, Thunderbird 2, was produced by Carlton as recently as 1999. Quite large, it makes an imposing addition to any display shelf!

and a collectors' card. They were capable of being used with Vivid's larger vehicles in the range (such as the Police Cruiser and Police Bike), and are now very collectable.

Harry Potter's Magic Begins

In October 1996, after six years working on her first novel, single mother Joanne Rowling received a contract from London publisher Bloomsbury. She received an advance of just over £2,000 for *Harry Potter and the Philosopher's Stone*, a book aimed at youngsters. Allegedly her literary agent warned her 'You do realize, you will never make a fortune out of writing children's books?' The following year, US publisher Scholastic Books secured the North American publishing rights, paying Rowling $100,000, somewhat contradicting her agent's views because this was a record payment for a foreign children's book.

Bloomsbury published the first British edition of *The Philosopher's Stone* in June 1997. The print run was small – only 500 copies. It sold out. As everyone knows, these first editions are worth a small fortune, signed ones even

more so. In the USA, the name of the first book was changed to *Harry Potter and the Sorcerer's Stone*.

Two more books, *Harry Potter and the Chamber of Secrets* and *Harry Potter and the Prisoner of Azkaban*, were published in the late 1990s. In 1999, Christopher Columbus was contracted to direct the first film, and three child actors, Daniel Radcliffe, Emma Watson and Rupert Grint, were selected to play Harry, Hermione and Ron; the film was released in 2001.

On New Year's Eve 1999, towns and cities around Britain held a series of major events to celebrate the Millennium. More than 4.5 million people were involved. A Beacon Project, resembling the burning beacons used in Elizabethan times to warn of the sighting of the Armada, involved 1,000 beacons around the British coastline and saw HM Queen Elizabeth II light the world's biggest beacon in London. Other events included high-wire walks, the opening of the ill-fated Millennium Dome at Greenwich and the Big Time Festival, a spectacular pageant along the Thames. For all of us, the year 2000 promised new horizons. For the legion of *Star Wars* fans, the dawn of the twenty-first century promised the final two pieces in a six-part jigsaw that had taken over a quarter of a century to complete.

RIGHT: A pretty common object only a few years ago, but soon even items like this figure of Lara Croft from the 2001 movie *Tomb Raider* will be scarce and of value to collectors.

LEFT: Before the new Captain Scarlet was released, the old-style superhero was perennially popular. This Vivid Imaginations action figure was produced in the early 1990s.

TWENTY-FIRST-CENTURY COLLECTABLE TV-GENERATION TOYS

What's Worth Collecting?

If we were each granted the wisdom of foresight, just think how many things we would do differently. Personal, professional and emotional matters aside, if we all knew in the 1960s that Corgi's Batmobile would be worth a small fortune in thirty or so years' time, we would have filled suitcases with them and earned a better return than on any similar financial investment.

Although we are perhaps still too close to any of the toy items produced so far in the twenty-first century,

we know from previous experience which items already released are likely to become an investment. So, what's hot and what's not?

The enormous success of the first *Harry Potter* movie and the others in the series that followed encouraged a range of manufacturers to bid for toy concessions. Hornby, the famous British toy train manufacturer, was one of the successful ones. Hornby released a number of sets, but one of the first, the Hogwarts Express Electric Train Set, is now very collectable. It came with a Harry Potter track mat and a Hogsmeade

In 1999, US manufacturer Revell produced a 1/25 scale replica of Austin Powers' Corvette Convertible from the Oscar-nominated movie, *The Spy Who Shagged Me*. It came complete with a miniature figure of Felicity Shagwell.

station halt, together with a range of other accessories designed to complete the scene.

Pierce Brosnan's last Bond movie was *Die Another Day*, released in 2002. In 2003 British manufacturer Corgi released a replica of Bond's Jaguar XKR Roadster. This miniature included rockets inset into the door panels and front grille, a Gatling gun, mortars and even spiked tyres. How's that for hardcore? At the time of writing, Daniel Craig, the new Bond and star of the latest instalment in the legendary series, *Casino Royale*, has been very well received by audiences. Indeed, early in 2007 this film was nominated for nine BAFTAS ('the British Oscars').

Okay, *Star Wars* fans … the really big news in 2002 was the release of *Attack of the Clones*. In this film, Episode II in the series and set ten years on from *The Phantom Menace*, Anakin Skywalker falls in love with Senator Amidala, whilst his teacher, Obi-Wan, uncovers a plot to assassinate her. This leads to the discovery of a secret Republican Clone Army. What it really meant for fans of *Star Wars*' creatures, gizmos and spacecraft was even more cool designs, and manufacturer Hasbro didn't disappoint, releasing lots of exciting licensed goods.

Amongst the huge range of figures and vehicles produced by Hasbro, a few personal favourites stand out. These include a really nice A-Wing fighter playset and blister-packed figure and accessory sets, one of my favourites being the Arena Conflict Accessory Set,

which featured a miniature Battle Droid (one of the most inventively designed *Star Wars* creatures), a jet pack and a highly detailed range of weapons.

My favourite *Attack of the Clones* toy from the Hasbro stable, however, is their weathered Anakin Skywalker Speeder, featuring 'blast apart' battle damage and mechanisms to allow youngsters to replicate the action of the film and actually see body panels fly off when 'hit'.

In 2005 Gerry Anderson's revamped *New Captain Scarlet* was a twenty-six-episode CGI-animated re-working of the original Supermarionation series first screened in the UK. Though purists will argue that you can't better the original, most fans would agree that this series is very watchable. Classic designs such as the Spectrum Pursuit Vehicle (SPV), Angel Interceptors and futuristic helicopters were updated.

Japanese manufacturer Bandai produced a range of high-quality toys licensed from the TV series. These included super replicas of the missile-firing Rhino, the Hummingbird helicopter and the Stallion bike, as well as figures to go with them.

Bandai also produced a large replica of the Skybase, the new Cloudbase. Because the manufacturer made replicas of many of the vehicles in both large and small scales, Skybase could accommodate the small-size Angel Interceptor fighters. Figures of Captains Scarlet, Black, Blue as well as Colonel White and Destiny Angel were also produced.

In 1993 Matchbox produced a superb replica of Stingray, as shown here alongside a carded 3in figure of Captain Troy Tempest. Even recently produced toys such as this are quite collectable. Well, they are from the Gerry Anderson stable after all!

I am sure that examples of the above and other licensed toys that were produced, such as a Captain Scarlet pistol set, are worth putting a way for a rainy day. We all know how valuable original toys released in conjunction with the original 1960s series are now.

Revenge of the Sith was released in 2005. It showed a maturing Anakin Skywalker finally giving into the dark side of 'the Force' and assuming the role of Sith Lord Darth Vader. This action-packed drama finally made the link with the first *Star Wars* movie of 1977 and showed how Darth Vader goes to war with his children, Luke and Leia. This film was full of fun and tied up lots of loose ends. We discover Yoda helping the Wookies defend themselves against the Droid armies on Kashyyyk and follow Obi-Wan as he chases the evil robotic separatist leader, General Grievous.

Hasbro excelled itself once again with a huge range of amazing toy collectables. However, amongst the many more serious items, including a neat General Grievous figure in the *Star Wars* Force Battlers series and Anakin's Jedi Starfighter (complete with opening canopy, retractable landing gear and spring-loaded wings that actually pop out at the touch of button), my favourites have to be the

ABOVE: **Boy band Take That was sensationally successful in the mid-1990s. In the same way as authentic Beatle souvenirs from the 1960s now command high prices, I am sure that things related to modern pop phenomena will, one day, also be worth top dollar. Take That's official annual from 1994 was purchased in the millions; it might never be worth all that much, but …**

… this 1994 limited-edition pocket projector, which allowed fans to see exclusive footage of Gary, Jason, Robbie, Howard and Mark in action, might well become quite valuable. At the time of writing, Take That is back on the road (minus Robbie) and attention is focusing on items associated with the band. So, who knows?

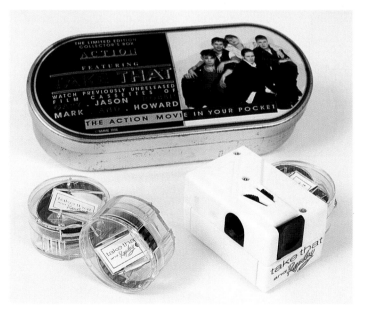

company's wonderful Playskool Mr Potato Head toys. Hasbro's stormtrooper potato head is great, but I reckon Darth Tater is destined to be a modern classic and very, very collectable.

Star Wars aside, there are lots of things that can still be found at car boot sales and on the dustier shelves of small toy shops, which I believe are eminently collectable.

RIGHT: **Another** *Take That Annual*, **this time from 1995.**

BELOW: **As with some Take That merchandise, this friction-driven Spice Girls Tour Bus, an official souvenir produced in 1997 and linked to their film,** *Spice World*, **is surely destined to become a collectable piece of twentieth-century pop memorabilia.**

The Official Take That Annual

SPICE GIRLS

Spice Girls Tour Bus
• Friction Power

SPICEWORLD THE MOVIE BUS

SPICE OFFICIAL MERCHANDISE

We all know how much items linked to quite transient fashions and pop groups from the 1960s and 1970s are worth today. So, in my opinion, it follows that products manufactured under licence to more recent super groups, such as the Spice Girls and Take That!, for example, will be worth a reasonable sum in the not-too-distant future.

It's very easy to think, when surrounded in a high-street store by seemingly hundreds of items licensed from a particular celebrity, TV show or character, 'This isn't ever going to be collectable'. I reckon that a lot of enthusiasts pass up opportunities of collecting potentially valuable items because they just seem, well … too commonplace. But though they might seem so at the time, there's a truism that all die-hard collectors understand – sooner or later those items are going to disappear and then, riding on a wave of nostalgia, their value will be rekindled but this time financially as well as emotionally. How many times have we thought: 'If only I'd held on to my …' or 'I should have bought a couple when they were on sale at half price in Woolworth's?

ABOVE: *The Totally 100% Unofficial Special* **(Spice Girls Annual), published by Grandreams in 1998.**

Beavis and Butt-Head Giant Inactivity Book **from 1998. It came with a 'handy remote control'. Creators Mike Judge and Larry Doyle's animated heroes from the Music Television Channel (MTV) are surely worthy of collecting and this very imaginatively presented book, especially so.**

I'm sure the toy collectables of the future won't simply be the *Star Wars* or *Star Trek* figures you would expect to be worth money, but also those toys and accessories licensed from more ephemeral programmes such as MTV's *Beavis and Butt-Head* or Trey Parker and Matt Stone's hugely successful animated show *South Park*.

It's a fact that products requiring manufacturers to pay a royalty to someone else every time they make a sale are generally in shorter supply than items they have either invented or developed themselves, or, like many cars, toys and dolls, are effectively based on objects within the public domain. My tip, therefore, is always to look for things, perhaps other than recent *Star Wars* items that everyone collects, related to short-lived films and TV programmes. Also, it's advisable to collect the kind of 'consumable' everyday things, like items of stationery, household products or cosmetics, which are often overlooked. Anyone in possession of original Beatles branded Biros, Monkees alarm clocks or *Charlie's Angels* eye make-up palettes are now in clover.

Before we briefly consider collectable toys and where to buy them in the next chapter, I thought it might be useful to list a run-down of the most popular toys so far this century.

The Toy of the Year 2000 was that little silver robot puppy Teksta, produced by Vivid Imaginations. That year, manufacturer Upstarts walked away with the Game of the Year with its Who Wants to Be a Millionaire board game, based on the phenomenally successful TV quiz show. Pre-school Toy of the Year 2000 went to Bob the Builder (HIT).

Bob the Builder walked off with the prize for best licensed toy in 2001 and *Robot Wars*, the popular BBC TV programme, which pitted rival teams and their home-built robots against each other, won Top Boys Toy that year.

Vivid Imaginations Spiderman action figure secured Boys Toy in 2002. The following year, the same manufacturer's Lord of the Rings range was voted Collectable Toy of the Year.

In 2004, nothing even vaguely related to a hit TV show or movie topped the polls of popular toys, with Bandai's Tamagotchi toys and Character Options' Robosapien interactive toy walking off with the top prizes instead.

However, in 2005, two TV- and film-related toys did indeed take the laurels. Both of them were a reflection on how children's tastes had changed and how much the design of components and features within toys had developed to satisfy them.

The British Toy Retailers Electronic Toy of the Year 2005 award went to the BBC-licensed Doctor Who Radio Controlled Dalek, while Hasbro won Boys Toy of the Year for its Star Wars Electronic Light Sabres.

Beavis and Butt-Head Annual from the late 1990s.

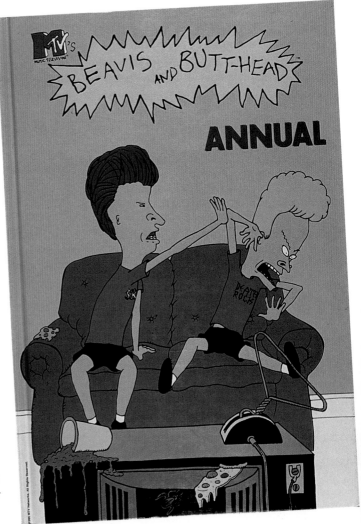

COLLECTABLE TOYS AND WHERE TO FIND THEM

The sad truth about toys manufactured in the last twenty or so years and marketed as 'collectable' is that they probably aren't going to be, or at least not as much as toys and games from the 1950s, 1960s and 1970s.

Here's the thing. Once upon a time, toys were bought to be played with. Upon receiving a new gift a youngster invariably threw away the packaging – the box was, after all, just a means of protecting the item whilst it was in transit from store to home. Die-cast

Flat Eric – The Famous Levi's Character. How many have survived the rough-housing of young children?

vehicles were regularly smashed into skirting boards – or into other die-cast vehicles. Many Matchbox, Dinky or Corgi vehicles wound up being played with outside, soon becoming grubby with garden earth.

They weren't precious; they were to some degree ephemeral. I remember with fondness my father painstakingly repainting many of my die-cast vehicles with Humbrol gloss enamel – because I wanted an alternative colour scheme. I still have these vehicles today and to me they are priceless; to a collector, they are probably worthless.

The couplings on Hornby toy trains often broke and the seemingly useless carriages were discarded. After a while, the tiny wire brushes underneath Scalextric racing cars became fluffy and the wheels clumsily wound with carpet fibres or hair, preventing them from rotating freely.

Airfix kits, until the last few decades always reliably inexpensive regardless of the series number, where routinely abused. Sometimes they fell from their lofty perches as the retaining drawing pins holding them to the ceiling gave way and they plummeted, trailing the dust-covered threads with which they were suspended. Goodbye propellers and aerials. Sometimes they were immolated as we naughty pyromaniacal youngsters discovered how well polystyrene burned (must have been all that oil we were told was the critical ingredient of plastic) and built funeral pyres of downed 'Spits' and Stukas.

Regardless of how well we looked after our model kits, they were invariably assembled, the kit boxes sometimes inverted as paint palettes or places to deposit the tube cement, transferring it to the model by cocktail stick.

We soon lost vital pieces for our board games. Useless, these too were generally disposed off.

The point is that only very weird kids kept all their toys mint and boxed. However, thirty or forty years ago Britain had more overseas possessions or commitments, or their fathers were in the armed services (like my dad), and many children were therefore packed off to boarding school. As a result, these children didn't have the luxury of being with their toys on a regular basis.

Thank goodness then, for the 'weirdos' and the army brats. The former kept their toys in immaculate condition and those of us whose life involved being marched in and out of new families quarters often saw a lot of their toys remaining in storage for years.

To be slightly more serious, I realize that an awful lot of the so-called 'mint and boxed' items survive simply because they were unwanted or forgotten stock that never left a wholesaler's warehouse and of course an amount survives as the result of bereavement. But the bottom line is that until old toys became an investment, and this really only started when vintage tin-plate

Dinky and W. Britains' hollow-cast soldiers began to appreciate in value in the 1970s, they were considered expendable.

I suppose Arthur Negus's antiques programme *Going for a Song* established a public interest in the value of old things. Hugh Scully's *Antiques Roadshow* quickly followed. Today, this veteran programme, now presented by Michael Aspel, regularly features old toys amongst its items – Bunny Campione being familiar to all toy collectors for her passion for toy automata, teddy bears and dolls.

The *Antiques Roadshow* is not alone. TV programmes such as *Flog It!*, *Cash in the Attic*, *Car Booty* and others conspire to show viewers how valuable previously commonplace items like toys can now be. The *Antiques Roadshow* even has a sister programme, the *20th Century Roadshow*, aimed at young people and with an emphasis on toys as recently as those manufactured in the 1990s.

Remember when, only a few years ago, you couldn't move without bumping into Cartman, Kyle, Kenny, Chef and the other *South Park* characters? Well, the brilliant show that was first aired in 1997 and its cast are still popular but sooner or later their popularity will wane. When that day comes, plush characters like this rather good figure of Eric Troy Cartman (who is voiced by one of the co-creators, Trey Parker), and some of the less salubrious creations from the show, may become extremely rare.

These programmes and a wide range of monthly publications remind collectors of how much an old Corgi toy or Airfix kit is now worth. Consequently, we now live in a time when people often take care to preserve the integrity of a child's toy, keeping the box, for example, so that the items can be reunited and saved for posterity. Knowing how much old toys, that 'we all had', are now worth and wishing that we had held onto our past treasures, many people now purchase two examples of a toy: one to let young Sammy play with, the other to keep.

Furthermore, today many toys, especially die-casts and even plastic kits, are marketed as limited editions, with the result that they are invariably treated with kid gloves. When I was young, very few people kept row upon row of die-cast cars in a glass cabinet. Today thousands do. The bottom line is that examples of a die-cast car that maybe 10,000 individuals world-wide

are preserving in pristine condition are never going to be worth that much. A Sean Connery 007 doll manufactured by Gilbert in the 1960s, of which only a handful survives, is always going to command top dollar.

But don't despair. There are things worth collecting. Some items by nature of the licence agreement within which they are manufactured are going to be produced in limited numbers. Some, more esoteric, items can be overlooked and consequently few are saved.

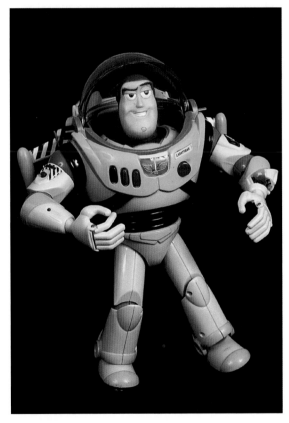

ABOVE: **Buzz Lightyear from Pixar's 1995 smash hit, *Toy Story*. Mint and boxed versions of early examples of this enormously popular toy are already exchanging hands for significant sums. I guess the irony of the toy collecting plot in *Toy Story 2* didn't escape the notice of the two films' creators.**

LEFT: **Another excellent modern item that I think is worth 'laying down' for posterity is Product Enterprise's retro radio-controlled Dalek (the BBC has a similar-sized version based on the most recent series in its range of licensed toys).**

These too can appreciate in value, especially the everyday items not immediately thought of as collectable. The recent sale at auction of Beatlemania period vanity sets springs to mind.

One dealer who certainly knows a thing or two about the value of kits licensed from film or TV shows is Tony James, proprietor of Comet Miniatures in London's Lavender Hill. I've known Tony for a long time. In fact, I first met him when he was essentially trading in second-hand kits. You could always be sure of finding that old Airfix or Monogram rarity amongst his stock. However, even in those early days it was clear to Tony and his customers that the money was in TV- and film-related kits, with an emphasis on science-fiction products.

As his business interests became more diverse and seeing that the future was in licensed kits and limited-edition collectables, Tony launched Comet Miniatures in 1989. Since then, it has greatly expanded on the same site. 'We produced our first model, a vacform and white metal kit of the *20,000 Leagues Under the Sea* submarine *Nautilus* and followed this with models of Stingray and Fireball XL5,' he told me. 'We then launched this country's first plastic kits of the TV and movie version Daleks. Our final in-house model was the *Blake's 7* spaceship, *Liberator*. All these kits are now discontinued and have since become sought-after collectors' pieces.'

Comet Miniatures now specializes in limited edition resin sci-fi kits as well as die-casts. 'I still have the enthusiasm and will continue to produce items that enthusiasts require,' Tony concluded.

Today, the first port of call for collectors of almost anything is the Internet. eBay led the way, of course, but since its inception there are now a plethora of online merchants conspiring to take your hard-earned cash in return for a 'must-have' collectable. Indeed, even I have to confess to an interest in this area, with the formation in 2006 of my online collectors' community, www.collectingfriends.com.

One of the real benefits of online purchasing is the ability granted by searching on a computer actually to see the objects of your desire. This is a far cry from the old days when dealers distributed typed lists of items for sale and you had to trust that the goods were as described. Although it's by no means perfect, the Internet mostly gives you the opportunity to see before you buy.

However, when you are looking for that 'certain something' online, do take care to check that the Corgi or Dinky item, for example, is actually of the vintage you are looking for. As we have seen throughout the pages of this book, unless restricted by a licence agreement, manufacturers have a habit of keeping profitable lines in stock for many years. The 'vintage Airfix James Bond and Odd Job' vignette you are offered might not be the 1960s original, but the one Humbrol/Airfix re-released in the 1990s. The box art was identical and really the only way of being sure in this instance is to see the packaging 'in the flesh'.

The one overriding advantage of the World Wide Web is its massive reach. Nowadays, from the safety and comfort of your own home you can literally view thousands and thousands of items. Frankly, if it still exists, you can usually find it online.

However, if you can't find it on the Internet, or are perhaps unwilling to pay the price asked, or are not prepared to wait for delivery (which can take some time if you are purchasing from an overseas vendor and have to wait for funds to clear and the inevitable delay of delivery), there's always the high street. Do remember, however, that most dealers have computers, perhaps originally installed for administrative reasons, but now, of course, connected to cyberspace. So they know what's what and are aware of current values for those most sought-after items.

Having said that you can find everything online, even in this huge marketplace certain items are becoming scarce and prices have risen. At the time of writing, I have noticed an increase in the prices asked for *Six Million Dollar Man* action figures, for example. *Knight Rider* star David Hasselhoff ('the Hoff', as he is known colloquially) has also been in the news recently. He's been on the West End stage and his records are still selling by the crateload – especially in Germany. Consequently, *Knight Rider* annuals and models of his talking car, Kitt, are becoming increasingly expensive. Along the same lines, I've noticed that items related to *Baywatch*, David Hasselhoff's other big TV series, are also appreciating in value.

So, back on terra firma: antiques and collectors' centres proliferate in almost every town. Lots of these are excellent, although some should revert to using the more honest name such traders adopted when I was young – 'Junk Shop'. Today, the majority of such centres seem to consist more of markets for a range of dealers who rent cabinet space within the premises. Although most of these sales rooms will entertain a discount of between 10 per cent and 15 per cent, they are in business to make money, so prices will be high – there are a lot of fingers in the pie.

Incidentally, Richard Ingram, a good friend of mine and the well-known militaria expert (he and I have a book on the subject published in this series by Crowood), once told me how to get the best deal. 'Flash the cash,' Richard told me. 'Let the dealer see that you've got real money, not cheques or credit cards, whilst you scrutinize your wanted item. Make an offer and when or if the dealer declines, walk slowly away. You'll be amazed how often the lure of ready cash causes the dealer to call you back and accept your first offer!'

Richard is right. The 'walk-away', as it is known, is a tried-and-tested method of getting a good price. However, all acceptable deals require the satisfaction of both parties, so don't be too greedy, otherwise you might walk away with a flea in your ear.

One place where it would definitely be improper and downright curmudgeonly to haggle is in charity shops. Don't gasp. I've heard many customers do so. Amidst the smell of old ladies' cologne and mothballs, which still seems to characterize these shops, there are often treasures to be found. And often at a very fair price, too. However, even charities have moved with the times. In order to quite rightly secure the highest prices for the second-hand items benefactors deposit with them, many charity 'brands' have taken to employing specialists to advise them on what is and isn't rare. Certainly, I have noticed that many of these shops are in danger of pricing themselves out of the market. Their prices for often quite worn second-hand books, for example, are becoming quite close to those charged by specialist dealers who at least try to ensure their books are in relatively good condition.

Two final locations where keen collectors can make great finds are the established car boot sales and collectors' fairs.

Car boot sales seem to be a phenomenon of the last twenty or so years. They have certainly changed since the earliest days, when it was possible to unearth real finds for a few pennies. These days, such fairs seem to be subjected to the early morning inspections of dealers who pick the rarest objects from the jumbled assortment, which is then left for visitors who would rather turn up after dawn. Still, they can be great places to find broken or incomplete items that can be purchased cheaply and later cannibalized to restore other old toys which are perhaps missing only a couple of hard-to-find parts.

Professionally organized toy fairs and the growing number of TV- and movie-related events dedicated to collectors of memorabilia and licensed souvenirs are not only great places to unearth that missing Action Man, celebrity autograph or *Star Wars* figure, they are also occasions to meet fellow collectors. Usually, specialist dealers attend these events, experts who are more than willing to offer advice to help you to gain the most from your collecting passion. They are, after all, fans themselves.

We collectors know that once bitten by the bug, we can't pass a charity shop, small toy retailer or, to be honest, even Woolworth's, without pausing to check if a licensed rarity lurks within. Nevertheless, regardless of where or how we get our fix, without us who would be preserving a tiny, perhaps insignificant (but I think important, however ephemeral) part of our everyday culture? Those who smirk at us are simply jealous that they didn't hold onto their *Thunderbirds* Dinky Toys or Louis Marx clockwork Daleks.

INDEX